Mealtime Recipes and Conversation

THE FAMILY TABLE

First printing October 1997
Canadian Cataloguing in Publication Data
Paré, Jean -
The family table: mealtime recipes and conversation
Includes index.
ISBN 1-896891-18-7
1. Cookery. I. Title.
TX714.P2738 1997 641.5 C97-900590-6
Published simultaneously in Canada and the United States of America by
Company's Coming Publishing Limited
2311 - 96 Street
Edmonton, Alberta, Canada T6N 1G3
Tel: 403 • 450-6223
Fax: 403 • 450-1857

COMPANY'S COMING PUBLISHING LIMITED

Author	Jean Paré
President	Grant Lovig
Vice-President, Product Development	Kathy Knowles
Production Coordinator	Derrick Sorochan
Design	Nora Cserny
Typesetting	Marlene Crosbie

THE RECIPE FACTORY INC.

Research & Development Manager	Nora Prokop
Editor	Stephanie With
Copywriter	Glen Wimmer
Proofreader	Michelle White
Test Kitchen Supervisor	Lynda Elsenheimer
Photographer	Stephe Tate Photo
Food Stylist	Stephanie With
Prop Stylist	Gabriele McEleney

BACK COVER PHOTO

1. Southern Raised Biscuits, page 14
2. Tossed Salad, page 114
3. Orange Sauced Beets, page 147
4. Steak Stew, page 74

Chairs, place mats, dinnerware and vase courtesy of: The Bay
Glassware, flatware and napkins courtesy of: Eaton's
Location background courtesy of: Creations By Design

DEDICATION

MAKE mealtime family time.

Company's Coming Cookbooks by Jean Paré

Company's Coming Series

150 Delicious Squares*
Casseroles*
Muffins & More*
Salads*
Appetizers
Desserts
Soups & Sandwiches
Holiday Entertaining*
Cookies
Vegetables
Main Courses
Pasta*
Cakes
Barbecues*
Dinners of the World
Lunches*
Pies*
Light Recipes*
Microwave Cooking*
Preserves*
Light Casseroles*
Chicken, Etc.*
Kids Cooking*
Fish & Seafood*
Breads*
Meatless Cooking*
Cooking for Two*
Breakfasts & Brunches*
(April 1998)

* *Also available in French*

Pint Size Books

Finger Food
Party Planning
Buffets
Baking Delights
Chocolate
Beverages (October 1997)

Hard Cover Series

Company's Coming for Christmas

CONTENTS

The Jean Paré Story 6

Foreword 8

Breads & Quickbreads 10

Breakfasts 18

Cakes 24

Cookies 33

Desserts 42

Main Courses 54

Pies 98

Salads 109

Sandwiches 116

Soups 122

Squares 131

Vegetables 146

Measurement Tables 155

Index 156

Mail Order Form 159

Gift Giving Coupon 160

THE JEAN PARÉ STORY

JEAN PARÉ GREW UP UNDERSTANDING that the combination of family, friends and home cooking is the essence of a good life. From her mother she learned to appreciate good cooking, while her father praised even her earliest attempts. When she left home she took with her many acquired family recipes, her love of cooking and her intriguing desire to read recipe books like novels!

In 1963, when her four children had all reached school age, Jean volunteered to cater to the 50th anniversary of the Vermilion School of Agriculture, now Lakeland College. Working out of her home, Jean prepared a dinner for over 1000 people which launched a flourishing catering operation that continued for over eighteen years. During that time she was provided with countless opportunities to test new ideas with immediate feedback—resulting in empty plates and contented customers! Whether preparing cocktail sandwiches for a house party or serving a hot meal for 1500 people, Jean Paré earned a reputation for good food, courteous service and reasonable prices.

"Why don't you write a cookbook?" Time and again, as requests for her recipes mounted, Jean was asked that question. Jean's response was to team up with her son, Grant Lovig, in the fall of 1980 to form Company's Coming Publishing Limited. April 14, 1981, marked the debut of *150 Delicious Squares*, the first Company's Coming

cookbook in what soon would become Canada's most popular cookbook series. By 1995, sales had surpassed ten million cookbooks.

Jean Paré's operation has grown from the early days of working out of a spare bedroom in her home to operating a large and fully equipped test kitchen in Vermilion, Alberta, near the home she and her husband Larry built. Full-time staff has grown steadily to include marketing personnel located in major cities across Canada plus selected U.S. markets. Home Office is located in Edmonton, Alberta where distribution, accounting and administration functions are headquartered in the company's own 20,000 square foot facility. Growth continues with the recent addition of the Recipe Factory, a 2700 square foot test kitchen and photography studio located in Edmonton.

Company's Coming cookbooks are now distributed throughout Canada and the United States plus numerous overseas markets, all under the guidance of Jean's daughter, Gail Lovig. The series is published in English and French, plus a Spanish language edition is available in Mexico. Familiar and trusted Company's Coming-style recipes are now available in a variety of formats in addition to the bestselling soft cover series.

Jean Paré's approach to cooking has always called for quick and easy recipes using everyday ingredients. She continues to gain new supporters by adhering to what she calls "the golden rule of cooking": never share a recipe you wouldn't use yourself. It's an approach that works—ten million times over!

FOREWORD

WHEN I WAS GROWING UP we always ate our meals at the table. It was a family affair. My two brothers, my sister and I all helped with the preparation and clean-up. Even though my mom worked in the family business, she was often home for lunch and always got home in time for supper with the family.

Conversation came very naturally to our entire family and it was nurtured at our table. We laughed a lot and I enjoyed bringing jokes and stories home from school to share with my family. Everyone was included in the conversation.

As I watch the families of my children and grandchildren grow, I see they have new challenges that I never experienced as a child. There have been many changes in the fabric of today's families that can be summarized in one observation: the fast pace we live is taking away from our time together.

The typical family today has two incomes and the average work week is stretching. Many parents are working harder and harder to make ends meet. When we are not at work, there are never-ending meetings and after-school activities of every kind for the children. One of the first concessions we make is to shorten the family dinner hour or dismiss it altogether with, "I'll eat later," or "I'll grab something on the way." Who could disagree that families today spend less time together than the families of the 1950s? This shift in focus is causing us to lose a deep-rooted and cherished force in family life.

Today, mail and the assorted trappings of everyday life tend to clutter our tables. It's time we cleared those tables and returned them to the important role of developing stronger families. Mealtimes provide some of the best opportunities for family building. Breakfast, lunch, dinner—anytime is family time when we can sit together for a meal. It is not a time for criticism, but a time for sharing, planning and discussion. Sitting across from one another at mealtime, family members can share their thoughts and experiences in an atmosphere of trust. Children learn about manners and the values we cherish. The opportunities for great conversations, fun and laughter are as numerous as the foods we eat.

Keeping things simple will return the greatest value to your family. Start by turning off the television when your family gathers at the table. Focus on each other, not outside distractions. Involve everyone in the conversation, adults and children alike.

This book is filled with mealtime recipes and conversation starters intended to help you bring your family back to the table at mealtime. The nourishment you receive will be far more than just what the body requires.

—Jean Paré

EACH RECIPE HAS BEEN ANALYZED using the most updated version of the Canadian Nutrient File from Health and Welfare Canada, which is based upon the United States Department of Agriculture (USDA) Nutrient Data Base. Some of the recipes use light, low-fat, or non-fat products. We encourage you to substitute your preference in any of these recipes. Our analysis is based on the first ingredient listed, does not include any optional ingredients, and uses 1% milk.

Margaret Ng, B.Sc. (Hon.), M.A.
Registered Dietitian

BREADS & QUICKBREADS

Everyone loves the smell of baked bread in the oven. The family won't be able to stay away from the kitchen. There is a place for breads and quickbreads at any meal whether it's breakfast, lunch, dinner or in between. All of these recipes can be made ahead and frozen. Serve with whole or sliced fruit for a quick dessert.

COCOA DATE LOAF

A moist loaf and a good keeper.

Chopped pitted dates	1¼ cups	300 mL
Boiling water	1 cup	250 mL
Baking soda	1 tsp.	5 mL
Butter or hard margarine, softened	2 tbsp.	30 mL
Granulated sugar	¾ cup	175 mL
Large egg	1	1
Vanilla	1 tsp.	5 mL
All-purpose flour	1¾ cups	425 mL
Cocoa	3 tbsp.	50 mL
Salt	¼ tsp.	1 mL
Chopped walnuts (optional)	½ cup	125 mL

Place dates in bowl. Add boiling water and baking soda. Stir. Set aside.

Cream butter and sugar together well in bowl. Beat in egg and vanilla. Add date mixture. Stir.

Add flour, cocoa and salt. Stir to moisten.

(continued on next page)

Stir in walnuts. Turn into greased 9 x 5 x 3 inch (22 x 12 x 7 cm) loaf pan. Bake in center of 350°F (175°C) oven for about 60 minutes. A wooden pick inserted in center should come out clean. Let stand for 15 minutes. Turn out onto rack to cool. Cuts into 18 to 20 slices.

1 slice contains: 122 Calories (509 kJ); 1.7 g Fat; 2 g Protein; 124 mg Sodium

Timeless Traditions

Do you have a recipe that requires the exact measurement of ingredients so that too much or too little makes a big difference? It reminds me of how many ingredients go into a healthy family and how difficult it is to keep these ingredients in proper balance. A great way to explain some of the difficulties of parenting to children is to use this analogy of the recipe. It will lead to important conversations about the balance between work and play, risk and security, and discipline and freedom.

Quick Biscuits

Serve warm for a snack or a meal and serve leftovers cold.

All-purpose flour	2 cups	450 mL
Granulated sugar	1 tbsp.	15 mL
Baking powder	4 tsp.	20 mL
Salt	½ tsp.	2 mL
Butter or hard margarine	6 tbsp.	100 mL
Large egg	1	1
Milk	⅔ cup	150 mL

Stir flour, sugar, baking powder and salt together in bowl.

Add butter. Cut in until crumbly. Make a well.

Beat egg in small bowl. Add milk. Beat to mix. Pour into well. Stir to form a soft ball. Knead 6 to 8 times. Pat or roll on lightly floured surface ¾ inch (2 cm) thick. Cut into 2 inch (5 cm) rounds. Arrange on ungreased baking sheet 1 inch (2.5 cm) apart for crisp sides, ¼ inch (6 mm) apart for soft sides. Bake in 425°F (220°C) oven for 10 to 15 minutes until browned. Makes 12 biscuits.

1 biscuit contains: 150 Calories (628 kJ); 6.6 g Fat; 3 g Protein; 191 mg Sodium

Pictured on page 35.

Timeless Traditions

Every time you make biscuits let your children take the scraps of dough and make figures like gingerbread men or their favorite animal. It's lots of fun to see their creations come out of the oven and creates memories they will never lose.

Banana Bran Loaf

How lucky - this is both good and healthy.

Large eggs	2	2
Mashed banana (about 3 medium)	1 cup	250 mL
Granulated sugar	⅔ cup	150 mL
Cooking oil	⅓ cup	75 mL
Vanilla	1 tsp.	5 mL
All-purpose flour	1 cup	250 mL
Natural bran	1 cup	250 mL
Baking powder	2 tsp.	10 mL
Baking soda	½ tsp.	2 mL
Salt	½ tsp.	2 mL
Chopped walnuts (optional)	½ cup	125 mL

Beat eggs together in large bowl until smooth.

Add banana, sugar, cooking oil and vanilla. Mix well.

Add remaining 6 ingredients. Stir to moisten. Turn into greased 9 x 5 x 3 inch (22 x 12 x 7 cm) loaf pan. Bake in 350°F (175°C) oven for 50 to 60 minutes. An inserted wooden pick should come out clean. Cuts into 18 slices.

1 slice contains: 124 Calories (518 kJ); 5.1 g Fat; 2 g Protein; 123 mg Sodium

SOUTHERN RAISED BISCUITS

Wonderful bread flavor.

All-purpose flour	2 cups	500 mL
Granulated sugar	4 tsp.	20 mL
Envelope active dry yeast (or 1 tbsp., 15 mL bulk yeast)	1 x ¼ oz.	1 x 8 g
Baking powder	2 tsp.	10 mL
Salt	1¼ tsp.	6 mL
Milk	1⅓ cups	325 mL
Water	1 cup	250 mL
Butter or hard margarine, cut up	⅔ cup	150 mL
All-purpose flour, approximately	3¾ cups	925 mL
Butter or hard margarine, softened	2 tsp.	10 mL

Measure first 5 ingredients into large bowl. (Yeast is not dissolved first.) Mix.

Heat milk, water and butter in saucepan until butter melts. Cool until fairly warm but not hot. Add to bowl. Beat on low to moisten. Beat on medium for 3 minutes.

Work in remaining flour until dough is smooth, elastic and no longer sticky. Turn out onto lightly floured surface. Knead 30 times. Roll out dough ¾ inch (2 cm) thick. Cut into 2½ inch (6.5 cm) rounds. You should get 24 circles. Arrange in greased 10 x 15 inch (25 x 38 cm) jelly roll pan. Cover with greased waxed paper and tea towel. Let stand in oven with light on and door closed for 1 hour. Remove to heat oven. Bake in 400°F (205°C) oven for about 20 minutes.

Brush tops of biscuits with butter. Makes 24 biscuits.

1 biscuit contains: 182 Calories (762 kJ); 6.9 g Fat; 4 g Protein; 216 mg Sodium

Pictured on back cover and on page 89.

Southern Cornbread

Makes a nice change. Serve warm with lunch or evening meal.

All-purpose flour	1 cup	250 mL
Cornmeal	1 cup	250 mL
Granulated sugar	1/3 cup	75 mL
Baking powder	2 1/2 tsp.	12 mL
Baking soda	1/4 tsp.	1 mL
Salt	1/4 tsp.	1 mL
Milk	1 cup	250 mL
White vinegar	1 tbsp.	15 mL
Butter or hard margarine, melted	6 tbsp.	100 mL
Large egg, fork-beaten	1	1

Stir first 6 ingredients together in bowl.

Measure milk in cup. Stir in vinegar. Let stand 5 minutes. Add to flour mixture. Stir.

Add melted butter and egg. Stir. Turn into greased 9 x 9 inch (22 x 22 cm) pan. Bake in 400°F (205°C) oven for about 20 minutes until an inserted wooden pick comes out clean. Cuts into 12 pieces.

1 piece contains: 175 Calories (733 kJ); 6.8 g Fat; 3 g Protein; 165 mg Sodium

Pictured on page 71.

Timeless Tip

The more different the personalities are within a family the more interesting the family. The same is true of this cornbread; the ingredients taste very different separately but when blended together, like a family, are a wholesome and nourishing food.

Kiwifruit Muffins

A different, moist muffin.

All-purpose flour	2 cups	450 mL
Granulated sugar	½ cup	125 mL
Baking powder	1 tbsp.	15 mL
Baking soda	½ tsp.	2 mL
Salt	½ tsp.	2 mL
Kiwifruit, peeled and finely chopped	3	3
Large egg, beaten	1	1
Butter or hard margarine, melted	¼ cup	60 mL
Milk	⅓ cup	75 mL
Vanilla	1 tsp.	5 mL

Stir first 5 ingredients together in large bowl.

Add kiwifruit. Stir gently. Make a well in center.

Add remaining 4 ingredients to well. Stir just to moisten. Fill greased muffin cups almost full. Bake in 400°F (205°C) oven for 15 to 20 minutes until an inserted wooden pick comes out clean. Makes 12 muffins.

1 muffin contains: 174 Calories (726 kJ); 4.9 g Fat; 3 g Protein; 226 mg Sodium

1. Egg Casserole, page 22
2. Pitcher Of Orange, page 19
3. Buttermilk Pancakes, page 21
4. Melon Salad, page 115

Glasses and place mats courtesy of: Stokes
Pitchers and china courtesy of: Enchanted Kitchen
Cutlery courtesy of: Le Gnome
Napkins courtesy of: La Cache
Vase courtesy of: The Bay

Breakfasts

The most important meal of the day is breakfast. Enjoy a sit-down breakfast with the family before the busy day begins. Make this the perfect opportunity to get in touch with what family members have planned for the day. Try setting the table the night before to save precious minutes in the morning.

Souped-Up Eggs

Soup makes a thick sauce in which to heat and serve hard-boiled eggs.

Condensed cream of mushroom soup	10 oz.	284 mL
Skim evaporated milk	½ cup	125 mL
Salt, sprinkle		
Pepper, sprinkle		
Hard-boiled eggs, halved lengthwise	8	8

Mix soup, milk, salt and pepper in heavy saucepan large enough to hold eggs in 1 layer. Heat, stirring often, until hot.

Add egg halves cut side up. Heat through. Serves 4.

¼ recipe contains: 259 Calories (1084 kJ); 16.4 g Fat; 16 g Protein; 773 mg Sodium

Pitcher Of Orange

Very refreshing for any time of day, especially for breakfast.

Frozen concentrated orange juice	6 oz.	170 g
Milk	1 cup	250 mL
Ginger ale	2 cups	500 mL
Granulated sugar	1/4 cup	60 mL
Vanilla	1/2 tsp.	2 mL
Crushed ice	1 cup	250 mL
Ice cubes, per glass	2-3	2-3

Combine first 6 ingredients in blender. Process until smooth.

Pour over ice cubes in glasses. Makes 5 cups (1.25 L).

1 cup (250 mL) contains: 153 Calories (642 kJ); 0.6 g Fat; 3 g Protein; 34 mg Sodium

Pictured on page 17.

Timeless Traditions

When my dentist had teenagers in the house everyone was so busy it was impossible to count on everyone having dinner together. The only time of day when everyone was home was breakfast. So they made this their "dinnertime" and there were no excuses for missing!

SPICY EGGBURGERS

Chili sauce adds zip to this burger.

Butter or hard margarine	1 tbsp.	15 mL
Large eggs	4	4
Salt, sprinkle		
Pepper, sprinkle		
Grated medium Cheddar cheese (optional)	¼ cup	60 mL
Hamburger buns, split, toasted and buttered	4	4
Chili sauce	4 tsp.	20 mL
Back (Canadian) bacon slices, fried (optional)	4	4

Heat butter in frying pan. Break eggs into butter. Prick each yolk with egg shell. Use a pancake lifter to extend yolk almost to edges. Sprinkle with salt and pepper. When showing signs of setting, turn eggs over.

Sprinkle with cheese, dividing cheese among eggs. Cover while cheese melts.

Spread each bun with 1 tsp. (5 mL) chili sauce. Add bacon and cheese covered egg. Serves 4.

1 serving contains: 275 Calories (1150 kJ); 14.4 g Fat; 10 g Protein; 437 mg Sodium

Buttermilk Pancakes

A wholesome nutty taste. Serve with a fruit sauce for a nutritious breakfast.

Whole wheat flour	2 cups	500 mL
Brown sugar, packed	1 tbsp.	15 mL
Baking powder	1 tsp.	5 mL
Baking soda	1 tsp.	5 mL
Salt	½ tsp.	2 mL
Large eggs, fork beaten	2	2
Buttermilk, fresh or reconstituted from powder	1¾ cups	425 mL
Cooking oil	1 tbsp.	15 mL

Measure first 5 ingredients into bowl. Stir.

Add eggs, buttermilk and cooking oil. Mix until moistened. A few small lumps are good to leave in. Heat heavy frying pan until drops of water dance around rather than sizzle in one spot. Grease lightly. Drop batter by ¼ cup (60 mL) measures into frying pan. If batter is a bit thick, stir in 1 to 4 tbsp. (15 to 60 mL) more buttermilk. When tops are bubbly and edges look a bit dry, turn to brown other side. No need to grease pan again. Makes 16 pancakes about 4½ inch (11 cm) size each.

1 pancake contains: 86 Calories (359 kJ); 2 g Fat; 4 g Protein; 210 mg Sodium

Pictured on page 17.

Timeless Traditions

In many households, it is traditional for Dad to cook breakfast on the weekends. It gives Mom a chance to sleep late and Dad gets to spend some quality time with the kids while they help him prepare these tasty pancakes.

Egg Casserole

Serve with toast on the side or over toast. Add a fruit salad to complete.

Bacon slices	8	8
All-purpose flour	3 tbsp.	50 mL
Dried sweet basil	1/4 tsp.	1 mL
Ground thyme	1/4 tsp.	1 mL
Garlic powder	1/8 tsp.	0.5 mL
Parsley flakes	1/4 tsp.	1 mL
Salt	1/4 tsp.	1 mL
Milk	1 1/2 cups	375 mL
Grated medium or sharp Cheddar cheese	1 1/2 cups	375 mL
Hard-boiled eggs, thinly sliced	8	8
Topping		
Butter or hard margarine	2 tbsp.	30 mL
Dry bread crumbs	1/2 cup	125 mL

Sauté bacon until crispy. Cut or crumble into small pieces. Set aside.

Mix next 6 ingredients in saucepan.

Add milk, a little at a time, while mixing well so no lumps remain. Heat and stir until mixture boils and thickens.

Add cheese. Stir to melt. Remove from heat. Spoon enough sauce into greased 8 x 8 inch (20 x 20 cm) casserole just to cover bottom. Add layer of 1/2 egg slices. Sprinkle with bacon. Spoon over 1/2 of remaining sauce. Add layer of second 1/2 egg slices. Cover with remaining sauce.

TOPPING: Melt butter in saucepan. Add bread crumbs. Stir. Spread over top. Bake, uncovered, in 350°F (175°C) oven for about 30 minutes until bubbly hot. Serves 6.

1/6 recipe contains: 386 Calories (1616 kJ); 26.2 g Fat; 22 g Protein; 658 mg Sodium

Pictured on page 17.

Spicy Applesauce

Serve warm over waffles or pancakes or serve as a fruit.

Cooking apples, peeled, seeded and cut up (McIntosh is good)	4	4
Raisins	¼ cup	60 mL
Ground cinnamon	¼ tsp.	1 mL
Salt, just a pinch		
Water	½ cup	125 mL
Brown sugar, packed or granulated sugar	¼ cup	60 mL

Place first 5 ingredients in saucepan. Cover. Bring to a boil. Reduce heat and simmer for about 15 minutes until apples are tender. Remove from heat.

Stir in sugar adding a bit more to taste if needed. Makes 2 cups (500 mL).

¼ cup (60 mL) contains: 79 Calories (329 kJ); 0.2 g Fat; trace Protein; 3 mg Sodium

Timeless Traditions

Breakfast night is a fun tradition for many families. Come to the table dressed in your bathrobe and slippers, as if it was morning. Have pancakes, eggs, or even cereal and toast. Younger children think this is great fun.

Cakes

The best way to polish off a great family dinner is with a cake. Make every family meal an excuse to celebrate. While the cake is baking in the oven, have other family members help make the icing. When it's time to ice the cooled cake, make sure little fingers stay out of the bowl until the job is done. All of these recipes freeze well. If you find a whole cake is too much, cut in half when it has cooled. Freeze one half and ice the other. Remember to freeze half the icing too!

Chocolate Icing

Good on any cake. Also good on a teaspoon.

Icing (confectioner's) sugar	2½ cups	625 mL
Cocoa	⅓ cup	75 mL
Butter or hard margarine, softened	¼ cup	60 mL
Vanilla	1 tsp.	5 mL
Water or coffee	¼ cup	60 mL

Measure all 5 ingredients into bowl. Beat slowly to moisten. Beat well until blended adding a bit more icing sugar or liquid to make proper spreading consistency. Makes 1¾ cups (425 mL).

2 tbsp. (30 mL) contain: 116 Calories (484 kJ); 3.5 g Fat; trace Protein; 35 mg Sodium

Chocolate Cake

Just the way families like cake. You get some icing with every bite.

Hot water	½ cup	125 mL
Cocoa	½ cup	125 mL
Butter or hard margarine, softened	½ cup	125 mL
Granulated sugar	1½ cups	375 mL
Large eggs	2	2
Vanilla	1 tsp.	5 mL
Sour milk (1 tbsp., 15 mL white vinegar plus milk)	1 cup	250 mL
All-purpose flour	2 cups	500 mL
Baking soda	1 tsp.	5 mL
Salt	½ tsp.	2 mL

Pour hot water over cocoa in large bowl. Stir until smooth.

Add remaining 8 ingredients. Beat on low to moisten. Beat on medium until smooth. Pour batter into greased 9 x 13 inch (22 x 33 cm) pan. Bake in 350°F (175°C) oven for about 30 minutes. An inserted wooden pick should come out clean. Cool. Ice with *Chocolate Icing*, page 24. Cuts into 24 pieces.

1 piece with icing contains: 212 Calories (887 kJ); 7 g Fat; 3 g Protein; 187 mg Sodium

Get Talkin'

Once in a while, encourage a different family member to invite a friend to dinner. A new face at the table will stimulate new conversation. It is fun to ask guests about their own family mealtime traditions. There is no limit to the uniqueness of each family's table.

Dated Cake

Chocolate chips and walnuts form the topping. No icing is required. A good keeper.

Chopped pitted dates	1 cup	250 mL
Boiling water	1 cup	250 mL
Large eggs	2	2
Granulated sugar	1 cup	250 mL
Butter or hard margarine, softened	1 cup	250 mL
Vanilla	1 tsp.	5 mL
All-purpose flour	1½ cups	375 mL
Baking soda	1 tsp.	5 mL
Salt	1 tsp.	5 mL
Semisweet chocolate chips	1 cup	250 mL
Chopped walnuts	1 cup	250 mL

Combine dates and boiling water in small bowl. Let stand.

Beat eggs together in medium bowl until frothy. Add sugar, butter and vanilla. Beat well.

Add flour, baking soda and salt. Stir to moisten. Add date mixture. Stir. Turn into greased 9 x 13 inch (22 x 33 cm) pan.

Sprinkle with chocolate chips and walnuts. Bake in 350°F (175°C) oven for about 25 minutes. Cuts into 24 pieces.

1 piece contains: 233 Calories (975 kJ); 14.7 g Fat; 3 g Protein; 260 mg Sodium

Lemon Cake

An easy cake from the shelf.

White cake mix, 2 layer size	1	1
Lemon-flavored gelatin (jelly powder)	3 oz.	85 g
Water	1 cup	250 mL
Cooking oil	½ cup	125 mL
Large eggs	4	4
Lemon Icing		
Icing (confectioner's) sugar	2½ cups	625 mL
Butter or hard margarine, softened	6 tbsp.	100 mL
Lemon juice, fresh or bottled	2 tbsp.	30 mL
Vanilla	¼ tsp.	1 mL

Put first 5 ingredients into large bowl. Beat for 3 to 4 minutes until smooth. Turn into greased 9 x 13 inch (22 x 33 cm) pan. Bake in 350°F (175°C) oven for about 40 minutes. An inserted wooden pick should come out clean. Cool.

Lemon Icing: Beat all 4 ingredients together in bowl until fluffy. Add a bit more icing sugar or lemon juice (or water if lemon flavor is strong) to make proper spreading consistency. Makes 1½ cups (375 mL) icing. Ice cooled cake. Cuts into 24 pieces.

1 piece with icing contains: 225 Calories (943 kJ); 10.8 g Fat; 2 g Protein; 121 mg Sodium

Timeless Traditions

I have never seen a child who was not proud to present the dessert at the end of a meal. Encourage children to be helpful in the kitchen by letting them help to prepare the dessert and to enjoy the universal tradition of licking the spoon.

Pumpkin Cake

This will fill your kitchen with a delightful aroma while baking. A large cake.

Cooking oil	1 cup	250 mL
Granulated sugar	1⅔ cups	400 mL
Large eggs	5	5
Canned pumpkin (without spices)	14 oz.	398 mL
All-purpose flour	3 cups	700 mL
Baking powder	2 tsp.	10 mL
Baking soda	2 tsp.	10 mL
Ground cinnamon	2 tsp.	10 mL
Ground ginger	1 tsp.	5 mL
Ground nutmeg	½ tsp.	2 mL
Ground cloves	½ tsp.	2 mL
Salt	1 tsp.	5 mL
Raisins	1 cup	250 mL
Chopped walnuts	1 cup	250 mL
Cream Cheese Icing		
Cream cheese, softened	4 oz.	125 g
Icing (confectioner's) sugar	1 cup	250 mL
Milk	1½-2 tbsp.	25-30 mL
Vanilla	½ tsp.	2 mL

Beat cooking oil and sugar in bowl. Beat in eggs 1 at a time. Add pumpkin. Beat to mix.

Add next 8 ingredients. Beat on low speed to moisten.

Stir in raisins and walnuts. Turn into greased and floured 12 cup (2.7 L) bundt pan. Bake in 350°F (175°C) oven for 55 to 60 minutes. An inserted wooden pick should come out clean. Let stand for 20 minutes. Invert onto rack. Cool.

(continued on next page)

CREAM CHEESE ICING: Beat cream cheese, icing sugar, milk and vanilla together until light. Spoon over top of cooled cake allowing some icing to run down sides. If icing a flat cake, omit milk. Cuts into 16 pieces.

1 piece with icing contains: 476 Calories (1991 kJ); 24.2 g Fat; 7 g Protein; 391 mg Sodium

Pictured on page 71.

TIMELESS TIP

Even today, wives and mothers are often the ones who are responsible for meal planning, shopping, preparation and cleaning. These tasks can be an ongoing burden. Get the rest of the family involved. Even small children can set the table and put away the dishes. The key is to make it fun and let your family know how much you appreciate the extra help.

Tomato Soup Cake

An old-time favorite.

Butter or hard margarine, softened	½ cup	125 mL
Granulated sugar	1 cup	250 mL
Large eggs	2	2
All-purpose flour	2 cups	450 mL
Baking powder	1 tbsp.	15 mL
Baking soda	1 tsp.	5 mL
Ground cinnamon	1 tsp.	5 mL
Ground allspice	½ tsp.	2 mL
Ground cloves	¼ tsp.	1 mL
Salt	½ tsp.	2 mL
Condensed tomato soup	10 oz.	284 mL
Prepared orange juice	¼ cup	60 mL
Raisins	½ cup	125 mL
Chopped walnuts (optional)	½ cup	125 mL
Cream Cheese Icing, page 28		

Cream butter and sugar together in large bowl. Beat in eggs 1 at a time.

Combine next 7 ingredients in small bowl.

Add flour mixture to sugar mixture in 3 additions alternately with soup and orange juice, in 2 additions, beginning and ending with flour mixture.

Stir in raisins and walnuts. Turn into greased and floured 12 cup (2.7) bundt pan. Bake in 350°F (175°C) oven for about 55 minutes. An inserted wooden pick should come out clean. Let stand for 20 minutes. Remove from pan.

Ice with *Cream Cheese Icing*. Cuts into 16 pieces.

1 piece with icing contains: 262 Calories (1098 kJ); 9.9 g Fat; 4 g Protein; 400 mg Sodium

Butter Icing

The finishing touch.

Icing (confectioner's) sugar	2 cups	500 mL
Butter or hard margarine, softened	3 tbsp.	50 mL
Water	3 tbsp.	50 mL
Vanilla	1 tsp.	5 mL

Beat all 4 ingredients together well in bowl. Add more icing sugar or water as needed to make proper spreading consistency. Spread over cake. Makes 1 cup (250 mL).

2 tbsp. (30 mL) contain: 152 Calories (637 kJ); 4.2 g Fat; trace Protein; 43 mg Sodium

Timeless Traditions

Look for little opportunities to celebrate family life such as finishing a long school project, surviving the annual review, making the first "A" or simply improving a grade. Place the honored person's meal on a different plate and let him or her sit at the head of the table. It's an easy and special way to share the other's achievement and happiness.

Plum Cake

Cake is moist and keeps well.

Granulated sugar	2 cups	500 mL
Cooking oil	1 cup	250 mL
Large eggs	4	4
All-purpose flour	2 cups	500 mL
Baking powder	1 tbsp.	15 mL
Ground cinnamon	1 tsp.	5 mL
Ground cloves	1 tsp.	5 mL
Salt	1 tsp.	5 mL
Strained plums or prunes (baby food)	2 x 4½ oz.	2 x 128 mL
Chopped walnuts	1 cup	250 mL
Butter Icing, page 31		

Beat sugar and cooking oil together in bowl. Beat in eggs 1 at a time.

Stir next 5 ingredients together well in separate bowl. Add to sugar mixture. Beat on low to moisten.

Add plums and walnuts. Stir. Turn into greased 9 x 13 inch (22 x 33 cm) pan. Bake in 325°F (160°C) oven for 45 to 55 minutes. An inserted wooden pick should come out clean. Cool.

Ice with *Butter Icing*. Cuts into 24 pieces.

1 piece with icing contains: 302 Calories (1265 kJ); 15.4 g Fat; 3 g Protein; 142 mg Sodium

COOKIES

Have the whole family help make cookies – creaming, measuring, greasing or whatever. Reward them with the bowl and utensils to lick and, of course, a freshly baked cookie to eat! Now try to keep their hands out of the cookie jar.

DROP COOKIES

Complete with raisins. A bit crisp around edges.

Butter or hard margarine, softened	½ cup	125 mL
Brown sugar, packed	¾ cup	175 mL
Large egg	1	1
Vanilla	¾ tsp.	4 mL
All-purpose flour	1¼ cups	300 mL
Baking soda	½ tsp.	2 mL
Salt	½ tsp.	2 mL
Raisins	½ cup	125 mL

Cream butter and sugar together in bowl. Beat in egg and vanilla.

Add flour, baking soda and salt. Stir well.

Stir in raisins. Drop by teaspoonfuls onto greased baking sheet. Bake in 350°F (175°C) oven for about 8 minutes. Makes 2½ dozen.

1 cookie contains: 82 Calories (343 kJ); 3.5 g Fat; 1 g Protein; 105 mg Sodium

Speedy Chip Cookies

These cookies are a cinch to make using a cake mix.

Large eggs	2	2
Cooking oil	½ cup	125 mL
Brown sugar, packed	½ cup	125 mL
White cake mix, 2 layer size	1	1
Semisweet chocolate chips	1 cup	250 mL
Chopped walnuts	½ cup	125 mL

Beat eggs, cooking oil and brown sugar together in bowl.

Add cake mix, chocolate chips and walnuts. Mix. Drop by rounded tablespoonfuls onto ungreased baking sheet. Bake in 375°F (190°C) oven for 10 to 12 minutes. Let stand for 1 minute before removing cookies. Makes about 3 dozen.

1 cookie contains: 136 Calories (570 kJ); 7.9 g Fat; 1 g Protein; 52 mg Sodium

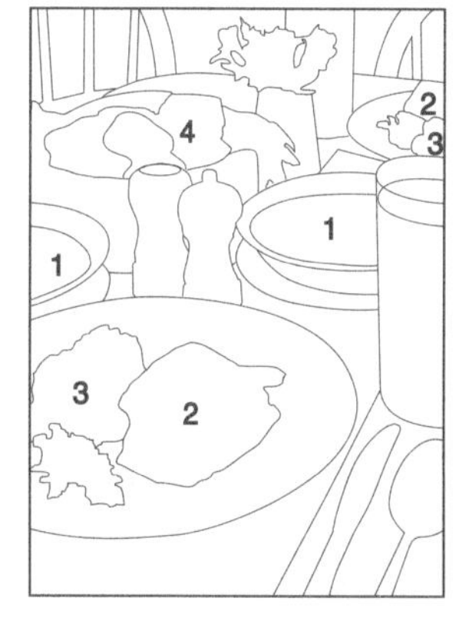

1. Chicken Noodle Soup, page 128
2. Crab-Stuffed Cod, page 84
3. Sauced Carrots, page 149
4. Quick Biscuits, page 12

China and glassware courtesy of: Stokes
Salt/pepper shakers and table runner courtesy of: Enchanted Kitchen
Vase courtesy of: The Bay
Napkins courtesy of: La Cache
Table and chairs courtesy of: United Furniture Warehouse

Sesame Cookies

Nutty flavored, soft and chewy.

Butter or hard margarine	½ cup	125 mL
Granulated sugar	1 cup	250 mL
Large eggs	2	2
Milk	½ cup	125 mL
Vanilla	1 tsp.	5 mL
Toasted sesame seeds (toast until dark golden)	¼ cup	60 mL
All-purpose flour	3¾ cups	875 mL
Baking powder	4 tsp.	20 mL
Salt	1 tsp.	5 mL
Corn syrup	1 tbsp.	15 mL
Water	1 tsp.	5 mL
Toasted sesame seeds (toast until dark golden)	2 tbsp.	30 mL

Cream butter and sugar together in bowl. Beat in eggs 1 at a time. Add milk, vanilla and first amount of sesame seeds. Mix.

Add flour, baking powder and salt. Work in to make a dough. Roll out ⅛ inch (3 mm) thick on lightly floured surface. Cut into 2¾ inch (7 cm) rounds. Arrange on ungreased cookie sheet.

(continued on next page)

Stir corn syrup and water together in small cup. Dab on each cookie so seeds will stick.

Sprinkle with remaining sesame seeds using a scant 1/8 tsp. (0.5 mL) for each. Bake in 350°F (175°C) oven for about 14 minutes. Makes 4½ dozen.

1 cookie contains: 76 Calories (318 kJ); 2.6 g Fat; 1 g Protein; 74 mg Sodium

Pictured on page 107.

Get Talkin'

Throughout the week, encourage different members of your family to take responsibility for the dinner conversation. Leading a family discussion that gives everyone a chance to contribute can be very interesting and rewarding. A little preparation before dinner can go a long way toward building nourishing conversations and mealtime memories around the family table.

SUGAR COOKIES

Colorful sugar-coated cookies. Small enough to try more than one color.

Butter or hard margarine, softened	½ cup	125 mL
Granulated sugar	½ cup	125 mL
Icing (confectioner's) sugar	½ cup	125 mL
Large egg	1	1
Vanilla	1 tsp.	5 mL
All-purpose flour	2½ cups	575 mL
Baking soda	1½ tsp.	7 mL
Cream of tartar	½ tsp.	2 mL
Salt	½ tsp.	2 mL
Granulated sugar	¼ cup	60 mL
Drops of red, green, yellow or blue food coloring (see Note)	8	8

Cream butter, first amount of sugar and icing sugar together well in bowl. Beat in egg and vanilla.

Add flour, baking soda, cream of tartar and salt. Mix. Roll into 1 inch (2.5 cm) balls. Arrange on ungreased cookie sheet.

Measure second amount of sugar into 1 or more containers. Add food coloring. Cover. Shake well to distribute color. Dip bottom of glass into sugar then press ball of cookie dough down. Bake in 350°F (175°C) oven for about 10 minutes. Makes about 4½ dozen.

NOTE: If 4 different colors are desired, use 1 tbsp. (15 mL) sugar and 2 drops of desired color. Repeat for remaining 3 colors.

1 cookie contains: 56 Calories (236 kJ); 2 g Fat; 1 g Protein; 86 mg Sodium

Raisin Date Balls

These look good on a plate with squares or cookies. Coconut covered with a crunch inside.

Large egg	1	1
Granulated sugar	3/4 cup	175 mL
Butter or hard margarine	2 tbsp.	30 mL
Chopped dates	1 cup	250 mL
Crisp rice cereal	2 1/2 cups	625 mL
Raisins	3/4 cup	175 mL
Flaked coconut	3/4 cup	175 mL

Beat egg in saucepan until frothy.

Add sugar, butter and dates. Heat, stirring constantly, until mixture thickens and dates are soft and mushy. Remove from heat.

Add cereal and raisins. Stir. Cool slightly. With greased hands, shape into 1 inch (2.5 cm) balls.

Roll in flaked coconut to coat. Chill on waxed paper. Makes about 4 dozen.

1 ball contains: 51 Calories (214 kJ); 1.6 g Fat; 1 g Protein; 24 mg Sodium

Pictured on page 107.

Get Talkin'

No one enjoys criticism and it causes most people to retreat and become quiet. This is particularly true with children. Stimulate mealtime conversation and friendly debate but make it a point to avoid criticizing anyone at the family table.

Oatmeal Cookies

A good kid cookie. Not fragile.

Butter or hard margarine, softened	1 cup	250 mL
Brown sugar, packed	1 cup	250 mL
Granulated sugar	1 cup	250 mL
Large egg	1	1
Vanilla	1 tsp.	5 mL
All-purpose flour	2 cups	450 mL
Rolled oats	1½ cups	375 mL
Baking powder	1 tsp.	5 mL
Baking soda	1 tsp.	5 mL
Salt	½ tsp.	2 mL

Cream butter and both sugars together in bowl. Add egg and vanilla. Mix.

Add remaining 5 ingredients. Mix well. Shape into 1½ inch (3.5 cm) balls. Arrange on greased cookie sheet about 2 inches (5 cm) apart. Press with floured fork or bottom of glass. Bake in 350°F (175°C) oven for about 15 minutes. Makes about 3 dozen.

1 cookie contains: 137 Calories (575 kJ); 5.8 g Fat; 2 g Protein; 135 mg Sodium

Timeless Tip

The next time you prepare the family meal, turn the TV off and watch what happens. Family conversation is more nourishing than any program on TV. When not fixed on the tube, your family will interact and communicate with one another much more.

Lemon Oat Cookies

Crisp and lemony.

Butter or hard margarine, softened	½ cup	125 mL
Granulated sugar	½ cup	125 mL
Brown sugar, packed	½ cup	125 mL
Large egg	1	1
Grated lemon peel	1 tsp.	5 mL
Lemon juice, fresh or bottled	¼ cup	60 mL
Rolled oats (not instant)	1½ cups	375 mL
All-purpose flour	1¼ cups	275 mL
Baking soda	½ tsp.	2 mL
Salt	½ tsp.	2 mL

Cream butter and both sugars together well in bowl. Beat in egg. Add lemon peel and juice. Stir.

Add rolled oats, flour, baking soda and salt. Mix well. Drop by rounded teaspoonfuls onto greased cookie sheet. Bake in 350°F (175°C) oven for 12 to 15 minutes. Makes 3 dozen.

1 cookie contains: 80 Calories (335 kJ); 3.1 g Fat; 1 g Protein; 87 mg Sodium

Get Talkin'

Dinner conversation is an art. It takes time to develop. There are two basic skills; talking, which is easy, and listening, which is often more difficult. There is an old saying that states that we have two ears and one mouth so we should listen twice as much as we talk.

DESSERTS

There is probably at least one person in your family with a sweet tooth for dessert. Indulge those who have stronger cravings with larger portions. Some family members can be clearing the table while others are serving dessert. To lighten some of these recipes, use a powdered topping or frozen whipped topping in place of whipped cream.

FRUITY PUDDING

Makes a quick and colorful dessert.

Instant vanilla pudding powder, 6 serving size	1	1
Milk	3 cups	750 mL
Sliced kiwifruit, oranges, bananas and blueberries (or other fruit)	2 cups	500 mL
Granulated sugar	1½ tbsp.	25 mL
Frozen whipped topping (such as Cool Whip), thawed (optional)	8-12 tbsp.	120-180 mL

Prepare pudding with milk as directed on package. Chill.

Stir fruit and sugar together in separate bowl until juice starts to run. Using 4 to 6 parfait glasses, layer ⅓ of pudding, ⅓ of fruit. Repeat.

Top each with 2 tbsp. (30 mL) topping. Makes 4 to 6 servings.

¼ recipe contains: 307 Calories (1283 kJ); 2.5 g Fat; 7 g Protein; 214 mg Sodium

Tampered Rice Pudding

A neat trick to make a different and colorful rice pudding.

Canned rice pudding	15 oz.	425 mL
Brown sugar, packed	2 tbsp.	30 mL
Ground cinnamon	1/4 tsp.	1 mL
Large egg	1	1
Canned apricot halves (or 2 fresh, halved and pitted)	4	4
Maraschino cherries (or 24 semisweet chocolate chips)	4	4

Stir rice pudding, brown sugar, cinnamon and egg together in bowl.

Place 1 apricot half, cut side down, in each of 4 custard cups. Spoon rice pudding mixture over top. Set cups in 8 x 8 inch (20 x 20 cm) pan. Pour hot water in pan half way up sides of cups. Bake in 325°F (160°C) oven for 40 to 50 minutes until set. Remove cups from water. Let stand 10 minutes. Turn out onto plates.

Add 1 cherry or 6 chocolate chips to each apricot cavity. Serves 4.

1 serving contains: 233 Calories (974 kJ); 5 g Fat; 6 g Protein; 103 mg Sodium

Berry Butterscotch

Fast to prepare, colorful and so tasty.

Instant butterscotch or caramel pudding powder, 6 serving size	1	1
Milk	3 cups	750 mL
Raspberries or strawberries, fresh or frozen	1 cup	250 mL
Granulated sugar	1 tbsp.	15 mL
Frozen whipped topping (such as Cool Whip), thawed (optional)	8-12 tbsp.	120-180 mL

Prepare pudding with milk as directed on package. Chill.

Mash raspberries. Sprinkle with sugar. Mash again. Divide pudding into 6 fruit nappies. Divide raspberries over top.

Add a scant 2 tbsp. (30 mL) topping to each. Serves 4 to 6.

1/4 recipe contains: 261 Calories (1092 kJ); 2.8 g Fat; 7 g Protein; 777 mg Sodium

Timeless Traditions

For one month pick a certain time each week, say Tuesdays at 9 p.m., and prepare a simple dessert to enjoy around the family table. How quickly your family will start to look forward to this "sweet time" will surprise you! This is a perfect time for each family member to discuss his or her plans for the next day and to put closure on today.

BREAD PUDDING

Custardy with browned bread cubes on top. Serve with Lemon Sauce, page 50.

Dry bread cubes, ½ inch (12 mm) size	4 cups	1 L
Raisins	½ cup	125 mL
Large eggs	2	2
Granulated sugar	½ cup	125 mL
Ground cinnamon	1 tsp.	5 mL
Ground nutmeg	¼ tsp.	1 mL
Salt	½ tsp.	2 mL
Vanilla	1 tsp.	5 mL
Milk	2 cups	500 mL

Mix bread cubes with raisins in greased 1½ quart (1.5 L) casserole.

Beat eggs together in bowl until thick and increased in volume. Add sugar, cinnamon, nutmeg, salt and vanilla. Beat well.

Add milk. Beat to mix. Pour over bread-raisin mixture. Bake, uncovered, in 350°F (175°C) oven for about 1 hour. Serves 6.

1 serving contains: 394 Calories (1647 kJ); 4 g Fat; 9 g Protein; 492 mg Sodium

Pictured on page 53.

REMEMBER WHEN?

Sometimes the family table is a place where parents can counsel children on ways to handle new situations, such as a new school or a first date. Sometimes it helps to tell a story of a similar situation we experienced when we were our children's age, complete with details of our failures and frustrations. Telling a true story about ourselves is a powerful food.

Baked Apple

Serve this quick and easy dessert with ice cream.

Canned apple pie filling	19 oz.	540 mL
Ground cinnamon, good sprinkle		
Raisins	3 tbsp.	50 mL
Chopped pecans or walnuts	3 tbsp.	50 mL
Butter or hard margarine, melted	2 tbsp.	30 mL
Granulated sugar	2 tbsp.	30 mL

Stir all 6 ingredients together in bowl. Turn into ungreased 8 x 8 inch (20 x 20 cm) pan. Bake in 350°F (175°C) oven for 20 to 30 minutes until bubbly hot. Serves 6.

1 serving contains: 190 Calories (527 kJ); 6.6 g Fat; 1 g Protein; 40 mg Sodium

Get Talkin'

Physical, mental and spiritual nourishment can all be experienced at the family table. Just as the physical food requires preparation, so does the mental and spiritual food of our minds. As a parent, when you are reading the paper or riding home from work, think of stories to share and thoughts to discuss with your family at the table.

Coffee Whip

Creamy color with tiny coffee-colored pieces throughout. Very different.
A light dessert after a heavy meal.

Envelope unflavored gelatin	1 x ¼ oz.	1 x 7 g
Water	¼ cup	60 mL
Boiling water	1 cup	250 mL
Instant coffee granules	4 tsp.	20 mL
Granulated sugar	½ cup	125 mL
Whipping cream (or 1 envelope topping)	1 cup	250 mL

Sprinkle gelatin over first amount of water in saucepan. Let stand 1 minute.

Add boiling water, coffee granules and sugar. Stir until gelatin dissolves. Pour into bowl. Chill until firm.

Beat cream in bowl until stiff. Using same beaters, beat firm gelatin mixture until it looks the size of grain kernels. Fold into whipped cream. Makes 3 cups (750 mL). Serves 4 to 6.

¼ recipe contains: 207 Calories (865 kJ); 10.1 g Fat; 2 g Protein; 14 mg Sodium

Get Talkin'

A fun way to get the whole family involved in the meal conversation is to have "True or False" night. Each family member comes to the table with three stories. Two of the stories are true and one is false. The rest of the family determines which story is false. The older the children are, the better the stories become and the more difficult it is to determine the truth.

Pear Cobbler

This topping offers a low-fat alternative to a pastry topping.
For more servings simply add more pears.

Canned sliced pears, drained, juice reserved	14 oz.	398 mL
Reserved pear juice	½ cup	125 mL
Lemon juice, fresh or bottled	½ tsp.	2 mL
Ground cinnamon	1/16 tsp.	0.5 mL
Granulated sugar	1 tbsp.	15 mL
Cornstarch	1 tbsp.	15 mL
Topping		
All-purpose flour	½ cup	125 mL
Granulated sugar	1 tsp.	5 mL
Baking powder	1 tsp.	5 mL
Salt	⅛ tsp.	0.5 mL
Butter or hard margarine	2 tbsp.	30 mL
Water (or milk)	2½ tbsp.	37 mL
Granulated sugar, sprinkle		

Place pear slices in ungreased 1½ quart (1.5 L) casserole.

Stir next 5 ingredients together in small bowl. Pour over pears. Heat in 425°F (220°C) oven while preparing topping.

Topping: Measure first 4 ingredients into bowl. Cut in butter until crumbly.

Add water. Mix in well. Press dough into circle to fit top of casserole. Place over pear mixture. Cut slits in top.

Sprinkle with sugar. Return to oven. Bake, uncovered, for about 15 minutes. Serves 4.

1 serving contains: 198 Calories (827 kJ); 6 g Fat; 2 g Protein; 158 mg Sodium

Chocolate Sauce

Spoon over scoops of ice cream for a last minute dessert.

Unsweetened chocolate baking squares, cut up	2 x 1 oz.	2 x 28 g
Granulated sugar	½ cup	125 mL
Skim evaporated milk	1 cup	250 mL
Vanilla	½ tsp.	2 mL

Put all 4 ingredients into saucepan. Heat on medium, stirring often, until melted and simmering. Reduce heat. Simmer, whisking constantly for about 20 minutes until smooth and thickened. Makes 1 cup (250 mL).

¼ cup (60 mL) contains: 228 Calories (954 kJ); 7.7 g Fat; 7 g Protein; 79 mg Sodium

Remember When?

Little children love their parents to ask questions about what they learned in school. My daughter would often ask her father, "Dad, would you ask me a question?" One night he asked her to name the Canadian provinces. Another night he asked her percentages of numbers. Sometimes, they would turn things around and my daughter would ask her father questions. She was so happy when she could stump him!

LEMON SAUCE

Excellent served over Bread Pudding, page 45.

Granulated sugar	¾ cup	175 mL
Cornstarch	2 tbsp.	30 mL
Grated lemon peel	1½ tbsp.	25 mL
Lemon juice, fresh or bottled	3 tbsp.	50 mL
Salt, just a pinch		
Butter or hard margarine	1 tbsp.	15 mL
Water	1½ cups	375 mL

Measure sugar, cornstarch and lemon peel into saucepan. Stir well.

Add remaining 4 ingredients. Heat and stir until boiling and thickened. Makes about 2 cups (500 mL).

¼ cup (60 mL) contains: 99 Calories (414 kJ); 1.5 g Fat; trace Protein; 15 mg Sodium

Pictured on page 53.

TIMELESS TRADITIONS

Numerous articles have been written over the past several years that discuss the valuable role that traditions play in helping family members to express what they mean to each other. The benefit of a simple tradition such as gathering around the family table, even if it is only once a week, cannot be overemphasized.

Bananas Caramel

Just a small amount of this sweet sauce is all that's needed. Scoops of butterscotch ripple or vanilla ice cream add even more to this dessert.

Caramel Sauce		
Brown sugar, packed	½ cup	125 mL
Butter or hard margarine	1 tbsp.	15 mL
Milk	¼ cup	60 mL
Icing (confectioner's) sugar	¼ cup	60 mL
Medium bananas, sliced	4	4

Caramel Sauce: Measure first 3 ingredients into small saucepan. Heat and stir until boiling. Boil for 2 minutes. Cool. Set pan in cold water to hasten cooling.

Add icing sugar. Mix well. Makes ½ cup (125 mL) sauce.

Divide bananas among 6 bowls. Spoon sauce over top. Serves 6.

1 serving contains: 167 Calories (697 kJ); 2.3 g Fat; 1 g Protein; 32 mg Sodium

Get Talkin'

Has life just been too busy to sit down at the table with the family? Perhaps one of you has been working late on a project for several nights and has missed the family mealtime. Gather the family around the table and try this dessert in a special time of encouragement and support. It could sweeten up a long day and relieve some pressure.

Instant Dessert

The quickest and the best.

Canned cherry pie filling (or blueberry)	19 oz.	540 mL
Butter or hard margarine	¼ cup	60 mL
Yellow cake mix, 1 layer size (or ½ of 2 layer size)	1	1

Spread pie filling in ungreased 8 x 8 inch (20 x 20 cm) pan.

Melt butter in saucepan. Add cake mix. Stir well. Crumble over cherry filling. Pat down gently with hand. Bake, uncovered, in 350°F (175°C) oven for about 35 minutes until lightly browned. Makes 6 servings.

1 serving contains: 351 Calories (1470 kJ); 13.3 g Fat; 2 g Protein; 237 mg Sodium

1. Bread Pudding, page 45
2. Lemon Sauce, page 50
3. Crispy Oven Chicken, page 58
4. Sauced Peas, page 146
5. Pineapple Slaw, page 113

China and vase courtesy of: The Bay
Glass salad bowl, sauce dish and place mats courtesy of: Enchanted Kitchen
Napkins courtesy of: La Cache
Tablecloth and cutlery courtesy of: Le Gnome
Cabinet courtesy of: United Furniture Warehouse

MAIN COURSES

These main course recipes suit any night of the week. Have family members who arrive home ahead of others chop and measure ingredients. The beef, chicken, fish, pork and pasta dishes will satisfy varying taste buds throughout the week.

CHICKEN ROLLS

A slight smoky bacon flavor is in the sauce. Rolling the chicken breasts is a different way of serving. If you prefer, they may be left flat.

Boneless, skinless chicken breast halves	6	6
Bacon slices, cooked, drained and cut in small pieces	6	6
Condensed cream of chicken soup (or mushroom)	10 oz.	284 mL
Non-fat sour cream (or regular)	1 cup	250 mL
Chopped chives	2 tsp.	10 mL

Pound chicken pieces flat. Roll up and secure with toothpick. Arrange in casserole large enough to hold in single layer.

Combine bacon, soup, sour cream and chives in bowl. Mix well. Pour over chicken. Cover. Bake in 350°F (175°C) oven for about 1½ hours until tender. Serves 6.

1 serving contains: 224 Calories (931 kJ); 7.5 g Fat; 32 g Protein; 590 mg Sodium

Fast Chicken Tacos

No taco could be easier or faster. Totally different.

Canned chicken, with liquid	6½ oz.	184 g
Light sour cream	2 tbsp.	30 mL
Light salad dressing (or mayonnaise)	2 tbsp.	30 mL
Chopped lettuce, lightly packed	1 cup	250 mL
Chopped chives	1 tbsp.	15 mL
Salt, sprinkle		
Pepper, sprinkle		
Taco shells	4	4

Mix first 7 ingredients in bowl. Makes 1½ cups (375 mL).

Fill taco shells using about 6 tbsp. (100 mL) chicken mixture for each. Makes 4 servings.

1 serving contains: 156 Calories (653 kJ); 8.3 g Fat; 11 g Protein; 293 mg Sodium

Timeless Traditions

Story night is a lot of fun. One family member starts a story and after a few sentences passes the salt shaker to the next person who continues the story. The shaker is passed from person to person with each one adding to the story until the last person finishes it. There is always a surprise ending.

Manila Chicken

Dark in color with lots of sauce left to serve over rice. Top of the stove dish.

Boneless, skinless chicken breast halves	6	6
Finely chopped onion	1 cup	250 mL
White vinegar	⅓ cup	75 mL
Soy sauce	⅓ cup	75 mL
Water	½ cup	125 mL
Granulated sugar	2 tbsp.	30 mL
Garlic powder	⅛ tsp.	0.5 mL
Salt	¼ tsp.	1 mL
Pepper	⅛ tsp.	0.5 mL

Arrange chicken pieces in large saucepan in single layer.

Mix remaining 8 ingredients in small bowl. Pour over chicken. Cover. Bring to a boil. Lower heat and simmer for 15 to 20 minutes until tender. Serves 6.

1 serving contains: 169 Calories (709 kJ); 1.5 g Fat; 29 g Protein; 2979 mg Sodium

Pictured on page 143.

Get Talkin'

Parents often shield their children from the troubles of the day. Sometimes it is good to discuss difficult issues with children so they learn at an early age that we all have our troubles. By sharing these troubles with our children we help them learn to face their own challenges.

Chicken Rice Bake

An all-in-one casserole. A salad or vegetable or both would enhance this. An excellent flavor.

Condensed cream of mushroom soup	10 oz.	284 mL
Condensed cream of celery soup	10 oz.	284 mL
Instant rice	1¼ cups	300 mL
Chicken parts, skin removed	8	8
Envelope dry onion soup mix	1 x 1½ oz.	1 x 42 g

Stir both soups together vigorously in bowl.

Add rice. Stir. Turn into greased 9 x 13 inch (22 x 33 cm) baking pan.

Lay chicken over rice. Stir soup mix. Sprinkle over chicken. Cover. Bake in 350°F (175°C) oven for 1¼ to 1½ hours until very tender. Serves 4.

1 serving contains: 463 Calories (1939 kJ); 16.2 g Fat; 35 g Protein; 2119 mg Sodium

Get Talkin'

As children get more comfortable with bringing issues to the table, be careful to lead them through to resolutions of their problems rather than simply telling them what to do. This process helps them build self confidence and learn to make decisions.

Crispy Oven Chicken

Crispy and browned just right. Pleasant blend of seasonings.

Large egg	1	1
Milk	¼ cup	60 mL
Salt	½ tsp.	2 mL
Pepper	¼ tsp.	1 mL
Corn flakes crumbs	½ cup	125 mL
Onion powder	¼ tsp.	1 mL
Celery salt	¼ tsp.	1 mL
Paprika	¼ tsp.	1 mL
Large boneless, skinless chicken breast halves (or use 8 regular chicken parts)	4	4
Butter or hard margarine, melted	4 tsp.	20 mL

Beat egg in bowl. Add milk, salt and pepper. Stir.

Stir next 4 ingredients together in shallow dish.

Dip each piece of chicken into egg mixture. Coat with crumb mixture. Arrange on greased baking sheet.

Drizzle each breast half with 1 tsp. (5 mL) melted butter. Bake in 350°F (175°C) oven for about 1 hour until tender. Serves 4.

1 serving contains: 270 Calories (1129 kJ); 7.2 g Fat; 37 g Protein; 722 mg Sodium

Pictured on page 53.

Saucy Chicken

A nice thick sauce is left to serve over chicken.

Water	2 tbsp.	30 mL
Cooking oil	1 tbsp.	15 mL
Brown sugar, packed	½ cup	125 mL
Ketchup	⅓ cup	75 mL
White vinegar	2 tbsp.	30 mL
Worcestershire sauce	2 tsp.	10 mL
Envelope dry onion soup mix	1 x 1½ oz.	1 x 42 g
Chicken parts, skin removed	3 lbs.	1.4 kg

Mix first 7 ingredients in bowl.

Arrange chicken, meaty side up, in single layer in small roaster. Spoon sauce over top being sure to get some on every piece. Cover. Bake in 350°F (175°C) oven for 50 to 60 minutes until very tender. Serves 6.

1 serving contains: 407 Calories (1704 kJ); 9.9 g Fat; 51 g Protein; 963 mg Sodium

Timeless Traditions

Once every few weeks, go all out with your family dinner. Use your favorite table cloth and put candles on the table. Use your favorite china or special plates. Let your family know that just being with them is a special occasion worth celebrating.

Chicken Burritos

A different burrito. Colorful, crunchy and good.

Cooking oil	1 tbsp.	15 mL
Boneless, skinless chicken breast halves	4	4
Flour tortillas, 10 inch (25 cm) size	8	8
Small head of lettuce, chopped (about 4 cups, 1 L)	1	1
Large tomato, seeded and diced	1	1
Zucchini, with peel, cut in slivers (7 inch, 18 cm, size)	1	1
Salsa (mild or medium)	1 cup	250 mL
Low-fat sour cream	⅓ cup	75 mL

Heat cooking oil in frying pan. Add chicken. Cook and brown both sides until no pink remains in chicken. Shred.

Spoon the following into each tortilla:

½ cup (125 mL)	lettuce
⅛	tomato
⅛	zucchini
2 tbsp. (30 mL)	salsa
2 tsp. (10 mL)	sour cream
⅛	chicken

Roll up tortillas, folding in ends. Makes 8.

1 burrito contains: 282 Calories (1179 kJ); 4.4 g Fat; 21 g Protein; 432 mg Sodium

Honey-Glazed Chicken

Nicely glazed with a delicious sauce.

Liquid honey	1/3 cup	75 mL
Prepared mustard	2 tbsp.	30 mL
Salt	1 tsp.	5 mL
Pepper	1/4 tsp.	1 mL
Curry powder	1 tsp.	5 mL
Butter or hard margarine, softened	2 tbsp.	30 mL
Paprika	1/4 tsp.	1 mL
Chicken parts, skin removed	3 lbs.	1.4 kg

Measure first 7 ingredients into bowl. Mix well.

Arrange chicken, meaty side up, in shallow baking dish. Brush generously with sauce. Bake, uncovered, in 350°F (175°C) oven for 1 1/4 to 1 1/2 hours until very tender, brushing with sauce every 15 minutes. Serves 6.

1 serving contains: 377 Calories (1577 kJ); 11.4 g Fat; 50 g Protein; 739 mg Sodium

Pictured on page 71.

Timeless Tip

One of the little ways to encourage a positive environment at the family table is to state criticism in a positive way. For example, instead of telling children, "Don't chew with your mouth open", say, "Please chew with your mouth closed," or "It's much better to chew with your mouth closed."

Chicken Rice Casserole

Add a salad and a vegetable for an enjoyable meal. If you're in a hurry, use the variation calling for instant rice.

Condensed chicken gumbo soup	10 oz.	284 mL
Water	2 cups	500 mL
Canned mushrooms, whole or sliced, drained	10 oz.	284 mL
Canned chicken flakes, with liquid	6½ oz.	184 g
Long grain rice, uncooked	1 cup	250 mL
Salt	¼ tsp.	1 mL
Pepper	⅛ tsp.	0.5 mL

Place all 7 ingredients in saucepan. Heat and stir until hot. Turn into ungreased 2 quart (2 L) casserole. Cover. Bake in 350°F (175°C) oven for 45 minutes until rice is tender. Makes 4¾ cups (1.2 L). Serves 4.

1 serving contains: 191 Calories (799 kJ); 4.8 g Fat; 14 g Protein; 1174 mg Sodium

QUICK RICE CASSEROLE: Omit long grain rice. Add 2 cups (500 mL) uncooked instant rice. Heat and stir until mixture boils. Remove from heat. Let stand for 5 minutes. Makes 5 cups (1.25 L).

Chicken Cheap Cheap

Cooking in liquid makes these economical thighs a good tender bargain.

Apple juice	2 cups	500 mL
Lemon juice, fresh or bottled	1 tsp.	5 mL
Seasoned salt	1 tsp.	5 mL
Garlic salt	½ tsp.	2 mL
Pepper	¼ tsp.	1 mL
Chicken thighs, skin removed	3 lbs.	1.4 kg

Combine first 5 ingredients in bowl.

Arrange chicken pieces, meaty side down, in small roaster. Pour apple juice mixture over top. Cover. Bake in 350°F (175°C) oven for about 1 hour until tender. Turn chicken over at half time. Serves 6.

1 serving contains: 321 Calories (1342 kJ); 9.2 g Fat; 46 g Protein; 339 mg Sodium

Timeless Traditions

Here is a suggestion to avoid the constant temptation to correct your children for their improper manners. Once or twice a month before the family meal suggest that this is "manners night" and everyone should be on their best behavior, parents included. How often children will catch their parents with their elbows on the table will surprise everyone!

CHICKEN PARMESAN

Simply coat with crumbs and bake. No need to turn chicken while cooking.

Fine dry bread crumbs	1/3 cup	75 mL
Grated Parmesan cheese	1/3 cup	75 mL
Parsley flakes	1 tsp.	5 mL
Poultry seasoning	1/4 tsp.	1 mL
Onion powder	1/4 tsp.	1 mL
Chicken parts, skin removed	8	8
Butter or hard margarine, melted	2 tbsp.	30 mL

Stir first 5 ingredients together in shallow dish.

Brush each piece of chicken with melted butter. Dip or shake in crumb mixture to coat. Arrange, meaty side up, on greased baking sheet with sides. Bake in 350°F (175°C) oven for about 1 hour until tender. Serves 4.

1 serving contains: 314 Calories (1315 kJ); 15.4 g Fat; 34 g Protein; 378 mg Sodium

TIMELESS TIP

We hear a great deal about "quality time" with children and may get the impression that this is a substitute for good old fashioned time. Simply being in the kitchen with children of any age can be some of the best "quality time" you will ever spend. You may quickly discover that "quality time" is "fun time"!

Lemon Chicken

Serve over rice. Add a vegetable and salad to complete the meal.

Boneless, skinless chicken breast halves	6	6
Lemon juice, fresh or bottled	1/3 cup	75 mL
Grated lemon peel	1 tsp.	5 mL
Sherry (or alcohol-free sherry)	1 tbsp.	15 mL
Soy sauce	1 tsp.	5 mL
Granulated sugar	2 tbsp.	30 mL
Water	2 tbsp.	30 mL
Cornstarch	1 tbsp.	15 mL

Heat non-stick frying pan. Add chicken. Sauté for about 15 minutes until slightly browned and no longer pink, turning over at half time.

Mix next 5 ingredients in small saucepan. Heat and stir until mixture boils.

Mix water with cornstarch in small cup. Add to lemon mixture in saucepan. Stir to thicken. Brush lemon sauce over chicken. Cover and simmer for 5 minutes. Turn chicken. Brush with remaining lemon sauce. Cover and simmer for 5 minutes until tender. Serves 6.

1 serving contains: 157 Calories (658 kJ); 1.5 g Fat; 27 g Protein; 135 mg Sodium

Creamy Burritos

Taste will vary depending on the strength of the salsa you use.

Cooking oil	1 tbsp.	15 mL
Ground chicken	1 lb.	454 g
Light cream cheese, cut up	8 oz.	250 g
Salsa (mild or medium)	1½ cups	375 mL
Frozen chopped spinach, thawed, squeezed dry	10 oz.	300 g
Whole wheat flour tortillas, 10 inch (25 cm) size	6	6
Salsa (mild or medium)	1½ cups	375 mL
Grated medium Cheddar cheese	½ cup	125 mL

Heat cooking oil in frying pan. Add chicken. Scramble-fry until no pink remains in chicken.

Add cream cheese, ½ of salsa and spinach. Mix, heating and stirring. Makes 4 cups (1 L) filling.

Place about ⅔ cup (150 mL) filling on each tortilla. Roll up, folding in ends to completely enclose filling. Arrange burritos, seam side down, in greased 10 x 15 inch (25 x 38 cm) jelly roll pan.

Spoon remaining salsa down length of each burrito. Sprinkle with cheese. Bake in 350°F (175°C) oven for about 25 minutes. Serves 6.

1 serving contains: 458 Calories (1918 kJ); 15.3 g Fat; 33 g Protein; 1454 mg Sodium

Pictured on page 125.

Chili Con Carne

So handy and so stretchable. Simply add one more can of beans.

Cooking oil	2 tsp.	10 mL
Chopped onion	1 cup	250 mL
Lean ground beef	1 lb.	454 g
Canned tomatoes, with juice, broken up	28 oz.	796 mL
Canned beans in tomato sauce	14 oz.	398 mL
Canned kidney beans, with liquid	14 oz.	398 mL
Chili powder	1-3 tsp.	5-15 mL
Worcestershire sauce	1 tsp.	5 mL
Granulated sugar	2 tsp.	10 mL
Salt	1 tsp.	5 mL
Pepper	1/4 tsp.	1 mL

Heat oil in dutch oven. Add onion and ground beef. Scramble-fry until onion is soft and no pink remains in beef. Drain.

Add remaining 8 ingredients. Heat, stirring often until mixture comes to a gentle boil. Boil slowly, uncovered, stirring occasionally until mixture thickens. Taste to see if you wish to add more chili powder. Makes 5 1/8 cups (1.38 L). Serves 4.

1 serving contains: 448 Calories (1876 kJ); 13.3 g Fat; 34 g Protein; 1878 mg Sodium

Pictured on page 71.

HAPPY DAY CASSEROLE

Use fyoo-SEE-lee for an interesting pasta. A fine looking casserole.

Fusilli pasta (about 1⅓ cups, 325 mL)	4 oz.	125 g
Boiling water	2½ qts.	2.5 L
Cooking oil (optional)	1 tbsp.	15 mL
Salt (optional)	2 tsp.	10 mL
Light cream cheese, softened	4 oz.	125 g
Low-fat sour cream	1 cup	250 mL
Chopped chives	4 tsp.	20 mL
Salt	½ tsp.	2 mL
Pepper	⅛ tsp.	0.5 mL
Lean ground beef	1 lb.	454 g
Chopped onion	½ cup	125 mL
Spaghetti sauce	1 cup	250 mL
Dried sweet basil	½ tsp.	2 mL
Grated medium Cheddar cheese	½ cup	125 mL

Cook pasta in boiling water, cooking oil and salt in large uncovered pot for 8 to 10 minutes until tender but firm. Drain. Turn into ungreased 2 quart (2 L) casserole.

Beat cream cheese and sour cream together in bowl. Add chives, salt and pepper. Stir. Spoon dabs here and there over pasta.

Heat non-stick frying pan. Add ground beef and onion. Scramble-fry until onion is soft and no pink remains in beef. Drain.

(continued on next page)

Stir in spaghetti sauce and basil. Spoon over cream cheese mixture.

Sprinkle with grated cheese. Bake, uncovered, in 350°F (175°C) oven for about 45 minutes until bubbly hot. Serves 4.

1 serving contains: 547 Calories (2289 kJ); 27.5 g Fat; 35 g Protein; 1128 mg Sodium

Timeless Traditions

Many young parents depend on their parents for keeping family traditions alive. But as the grandparents get older it becomes the responsibility of their children to create new traditions for their families. What would be a meaningful tradition in your family? Discuss the effect of traditions on the family. Do they give everyone a sense of comfort and security? Remember, traditions do not need to last forever. When they begin to lose their ability to touch and nourish your family, it is time to create new ones.

Beefy Rice Patties

A new version of half beef and half rice. Very good. A real meat stretcher.

Boiling water	1¼ cups	300 mL
Instant rice	1 cup	250 mL
Lean ground beef	1 lb.	454 g
Large egg	1	1
Worcestershire sauce	1 tsp.	5 mL
Beef bouillon powder	1 tsp.	5 mL
Salt	1 tsp.	5 mL
Pepper	¼ tsp.	1 mL

Pour boiling water over rice in bowl. Cover. Let stand for 10 minutes.

Add remaining 6 ingredients. Mix well. Shape into 8 patties about 3½ inches (9 cm) in diameter. Heat non-stick frying pan. Add meat patties. Brown both sides, cooking until well done. Makes 8. Serves 4 to 6.

¼ recipe contains: 362 Calories (1514 kJ); 18.5 g Fat; 25 g Protein; 934 mg Sodium

1. Creamy Greens, page 110
2. Chili Con Carne, page 67
3. Honey-Glazed Chicken, page 61
4. Southern Cornbread, page 15
5. Pumpkin Cake, page 28
6. Cream Cheese Icing, page 28

Dinnerware and glassware courtesy of: Eaton's
Pottery dishes courtesy of: Mystique Pottery & Gifts
Cutlery courtesy of: The Bay
Serving fork courtesy of: Stokes
Glass pitcher courtesy of: The Glasshouse
Napkins courtesy of: Le Gnome
Table and chairs courtesy of: United Furniture Warehouse

Burger Meal

Yummy burgers with golden fries.

Oven Fries		
Medium potatoes, peeled, cut in long strips	4	4
Cooking oil	1 tbsp.	15 mL
Burgers		
Lean ground beef	1 lb.	454 g
Dry bread crumbs	1/3 cup	75 mL
Water	1/3 cup	75 mL
Ketchup	1 tbsp.	15 mL
Soy sauce	1 tsp.	5 mL
Onion powder	1/4 tsp.	1 mL
Salt	1/2 tsp.	2 mL
Pepper	1/4 tsp.	1 mL
Cooking oil	1 tbsp.	15 mL
Hamburger buns, split and buttered	4	4
Salsa (mild or medium)	4 tbsp.	60 mL
Lettuce leaves, to fit buns (optional)	8	8
Tomato slices (optional)		
Thinly sliced pickles (optional)		

Oven Fries: Toss potato strips and cooking oil together in large bowl. Arrange on baking sheet. When ready to cook burgers, put potato into 450°F (230°C) oven for 15 minutes. Turn strips. Cook for 10 to 15 minutes more until tender.

Burgers: Mix first 8 ingredients well in bowl. Shape into 4 patties as large as or a bit wider than buns.

(continued on next page)

Heat cooking oil in frying pan. Add patties. Cook, browning both sides, until no pink remains in beef.

Insert patty into each bun. Spread with salsa. Add lettuce, tomato slice and pickles. Serve with *Oven Fries*. Serves 4.

1 Burger and 1 serving Oven Fries contain: 613 Calories (2564 kJ); 31.1 g Fat; 29 g Protein; 981 mg Sodium

Variation: Omit *Oven Fries*. Serve burgers with *Potato Salad*, page 112.

REMEMBER WHEN?

Everyone loves a good story and often grandmothers and grandfathers tell some great ones. When gathered around the family table ask the grandparents questions about their past that will interest your children and reveal lessons that may be pertinent to them. Often grandparents can best communicate our most cherished values to our children.

STEAK STEW

Add mashed potatoes or noodles to complete the meal.
Meat and vegetables are simmered in a frying pan.

Hard margarine (butter browns too fast)	1 tbsp.	15 mL
Round steak, trimmed of fat, cut into bite-size pieces	1½ lbs.	680 g
Hot water	2¼ cups	550 mL
Salt	¾ tsp.	4 mL
Pepper	¼ tsp.	1 mL
Coarsely chopped onion	1½ cups	375 mL
Sliced carrot	2¼ cups	550 mL
Frozen peas	1 cup	250 mL
All-purpose flour	1 tbsp.	15 mL
Water	¼ cup	60 mL

Heat margarine in frying pan. Add steak. Brown both sides well.

Pour water over steak. Add salt and pepper directly into water. Stir to mix. Reduce heat. Simmer, covered, for 1 hour.

Add onion and carrot. Cover. Simmer for about ½ hour until steak is tender.

Sprinkle with peas. Simmer for 3 to 5 minutes to cook. Remove steak and vegetables to serving dish.

Stir flour into second amount of water in small bowl or cup until no lumps remain. Stir into pan juices (add more water to pan if needed) until mixture boils and thickens. Pour over steak and vegetables. Serves 4.

1 serving contains: 320 Calories (1338 kJ); 6.9 g Fat; 43 g Protein; 710 mg Sodium

Pictured on back cover.

Porcupines

These rice "needles" aren't sharp. An oven-baked dish sure to please.

Lean ground beef	1 lb.	454 g
Finely chopped onion	⅓ cup	75 mL
Long grain rice	½ cup	125 mL
Beef bouillon powder	1 tsp.	5 mL
Salt	1 tsp.	5 mL
Pepper	½ tsp.	2 mL
Small green pepper, seeded and cut into strips	1	1
Medium onion, cut into wide strips	1	1
Tomato juice	2½ cups	625 mL
Soy sauce	1 tbsp.	15 mL
Brown sugar, packed	2 tbsp.	30 mL

Put first 6 ingredients into bowl. Mix well. Shape into 1¼ inch (3 cm) meatballs. Arrange in 8 x 8 inch (20 x 20 cm) baking dish.

Arrange green pepper strips and onion strips among meatballs.

Stir tomato juice, soy sauce and sugar together. Pour over all. Cover. Bake in 350°F (175°C) oven for 60 to 70 minutes until rice is tender. Makes 24 meatballs. Serves 4 to 5.

¼ recipe contains: 324 Calories (1357 kJ); 17.4 g Fat; 24 g Protein; 1731 mg Sodium

Pictured on page 89.

Ground Beef Stroganoff

Just the right topping to serve over rice or noodles.

Cooking oil	1 tbsp.	15 mL
Chopped onion	1 cup	250 mL
Lean ground beef	1 lb.	454 g
All-purpose flour	2 tbsp.	30 mL
Garlic salt	½ tsp.	2 mL
Paprika	¼ tsp.	1 mL
Salt	½ tsp.	2 mL
Pepper	⅛ tsp.	0.5 mL
Canned sliced mushrooms, with liquid	10 oz.	284 mL
Condensed cream of mushroom soup	10 oz.	284 mL
Non-fat sour cream (or regular or light)	1 cup	250 mL

Heat cooking oil in frying pan. Add onion and ground beef. Scramble-fry until onion is soft and no pink remains in beef.

Mix in flour, garlic salt, paprika, salt and pepper.

Add mushrooms with liquid and soup, stirring until boiling and thickened.

Stir in sour cream. Makes 4 cups (1 L).

1 cup (250 mL) contains: 339 Calories (1409 kJ); 18.8 g Fat; 25 g Protein; 1422 mg Sodium

BEEF NOODLE BAKE

Mild, mellow and pleasant.

Lean ground beef	1½ lbs.	680 g
Chopped onion	1 cup	250 mL
Water	1½ cups	375 mL
Tomato sauce	7½ oz.	213 g
Canned mushroom pieces, drained	10 oz.	284 mL
Canned kernel corn, drained (or 1½ cups, 375 mL, frozen)	12 oz.	375 g
Chili powder	½ tsp.	2 mL
Garlic powder	¼ tsp.	1 mL
Salt	1 tsp.	5 mL
Pepper	¼ tsp.	1 mL
Medium noodles, uncooked	8 oz.	250 g
Grated medium Cheddar cheese	1 cup	250 mL

Heat non-stick frying pan. Add ground beef and onion. Scramble-fry until onion is soft and no pink remains in beef. Drain.

Stir next 8 ingredients in large bowl. Add ground beef mixture. Stir.

Add noodles. Stir. Turn into ungreased 3 quart (3 L) casserole. Cover. Bake in 350°F (175°C) oven for 25 minutes. Stir top noodles down. Cover. Bake for 20 minutes until noodles are tender but firm.

Sprinkle with cheese. Bake, uncovered, for about 5 minutes until cheese is melted. Serves 6.

1 serving contains: 471 Calories (1972 kJ); 17.3 g Fat; 33 g Protein; 1112 mg Sodium

BAKED SPARERIBS

Once these are in the oven, they don't call for attention.

Pork back ribs, cut into 3 rib serving pieces	3 lbs.	1.4 kg
Salt, sprinkle		
Pepper, sprinkle		
Medium onions, chopped or sliced	2	2
Water	1 cup	250 mL
Ketchup	¾ cup	175 mL
Prepared mustard	1 tsp.	5 mL
Chicken bouillon powder	1 tsp.	5 mL
Cayenne pepper	¼ tsp.	1 mL
Garlic powder	¼ tsp.	1 mL
Soy sauce	1 tbsp.	15 mL

Arrange ½ of ribs in small roaster. Sprinkle with salt and pepper. Spread ½ of onion over top.

Mix remaining 7 ingredients in bowl. Spoon ½ of sauce over first layer of onion and ribs. Cover with remaining ribs, onions and sauce. Bake, covered, in 350°F (175°C) oven for about 1½ hours until ribs are tender. Serves 4.

1 serving contains: 719 Calories (3009 kJ); 48.8 g Fat; 49 g Protein; 1172 mg Sodium

Cranberry Pork Chops

Very tender and good flavored.

Hard margarine (butter browns too fast)	1 tbsp.	15 mL
Pork chops, trimmed of fat	4-6	4-6
Whole cranberry sauce	½ cup	125 mL
Squeezed orange juice	2 tbsp.	30 mL
Grated orange peel	2 tsp.	10 mL

Heat margarine in frying pan. Add pork chops. Brown well on both sides.

Stir cranberry sauce, orange juice and orange peel together in small bowl. Arrange chops in ungreased casserole large enough to hold single layer. Divide cranberry mixture over top of each one. Cover. Bake in 350°F (175°C) oven for 40 to 50 minutes until cooked and tender. Serves 4 to 6.

¼ recipe contains: 249 Calories (1040 kJ); 11.6 g Fat; 20 g Protein; 88 mg Sodium

Get Talkin'

A great conversation starter when teenagers are present is to have "CD night". Encourage them to play their favorite CD and tell the rest of the family why they like the music. Then, you as parents, play your music and explain why you like it. You can discover a lot about your family by understanding why they like the music they do.

Oven Pork Chops

No pre-browning needed. Roasted in the oven in an apple-flavored sauce.

Thick pork chops, trimmed of fat, ¾ to 1 inch (2 to 2.5 cm) thick	4	4
Apple juice	⅓ cup	75 mL
Prepared mustard	½ tsp.	2 mL
Worcestershire sauce	½ tsp.	2 mL
Brown sugar, packed	2 tbsp.	30 mL
Salt	½ tsp.	2 mL
Pepper	⅛ tsp.	0.5 mL
Cornstarch	2 tsp.	10 mL
Water	1 tbsp.	15 mL

Arrange pork chops in casserole or pan large enough to hold in single layer.

Pour apple juice into small saucepan. Add next 5 ingredients. Heat and stir until boiling.

Stir cornstarch and water together in small cup. Stir into apple juice mixture until boiling. Spoon over pork chops. Cover. Bake in 350°F (175°C) oven for about 1 hour until tender, spooning sauce over pork chops again at half time. Serves 4.

1 serving contains: 288 Calories (1206 kJ); 13.1 g Fat; 30 g Protein; 423 mg Sodium

Kids' Quiche

Contains potato, peas and wieners. The kids will love it!

Wieners, thinly sliced in coins	4	4
Unbaked 9 inch (22 cm) pie shell	1	1
Diced cooked potato (about 1 medium)	1 cup	250 mL
Frozen peas	½ cup	125 mL
Large eggs	3	3
Skim evaporated milk (small can)	⅔ cup	150 mL
Soy sauce	1 tsp.	5 mL
Prepared mustard	¾ tsp.	4 mL
Onion powder	¼ tsp.	1 mL
Salt	¼ tsp.	1 mL
Pepper	⅛ tsp.	0.5 mL
Grated medium Cheddar cheese	½ cup	125 mL
Paprika, sprinkle		

Scatter wieners in pie shell.

Add diced potato and peas over wieners.

Beat eggs together in bowl until frothy. Add next 6 ingredients. Beat to mix. Pour into pie shell.

Sprinkle with cheese and paprika. Bake on bottom shelf in 400°F (205°C) oven for 15 minutes. Reduce heat to 325°F (160°C). Continue to bake for 25 to 35 minutes until knife inserted near center comes out clean. Makes 6 servings.

1 serving contains: 362 Calories (1514 kJ); 23.3 g Fat; 14 g Protein; 787 mg Sodium

Baked Ham Steak

A quick oven dish. Sweet and sour flavor with a nip of mustard.

Apricot jam (or peach), mashed	¼ cup	60 mL
Low-fat sour cream	⅓ cup	75 mL
Prepared mustard	1 tsp.	5 mL
Ground cloves	⅛ tsp.	0.5 mL
Cider vinegar	1 tsp.	5 mL
Ham steak	1½ lbs.	680 g

Stir first 5 ingredients together in small bowl.

Clip fat edges of ham to prevent curling up. Place ham steak in baking pan. Broil for 5 minutes on each side. Turn oven to 350°F (175°C). Spread ham with sour cream mixture. Bake on center rack for about 20 minutes until mixture has set. Serves 4.

1 serving contains: 285 Calories (1192 kJ); 8.7 g Fat; 34 g Protein; 2187 mg Sodium

Timeless Traditions

The dinnertime traditions of your family are reflected in such things as the cutlery you choose, the use of paper or cloth napkins, and the presence or absence of candles on the table. Take time to recognize the uniqueness of your family table.

BAKED HALIBUT

Topping will remind you of a stuffing flavor.
A nice variation to serve with fish.

Fish steaks (such as halibut or your favorite)	2 lbs.	900 g
Cooking oil	1 tbsp.	15 mL
Butter or hard margarine	1 tbsp.	15 mL
Chopped onion	1 cup	250 mL
Soda cracker crumbs	1 cup	250 mL
Ground marjoram	2 tsp.	10 mL
Skim evaporated milk (or light cream)	13½ oz.	385 mL
Salt	¾ tsp.	4 mL
Pepper	¼ tsp.	1 mL

If steaks are large, cut in half. Brush with cooking oil. Arrange in greased baking dish large enough to hold in single layer.

Melt butter in frying pan. Add onion. Sauté until soft and golden. Remove from heat.

Stir in cracker crumbs, marjoram, milk, salt and pepper. Spoon over fish. Bake, covered, in 375°F (190°C) oven for about 30 minutes until fish flakes. Serves 6.

1 serving contains: 341 Calories (1428 kJ); 10.1 g Fat; 38 g Protein; 704 mg Sodium

Variation: Top with a few slivers of red pepper or pimiento for added color.

Crab-Stuffed Cod

A special dish yet easy to prepare.

Stuffing		
Butter or hard margarine	1 tbsp.	15 mL
Chopped onion	1/3 cup	75 mL
Chopped celery	2 tbsp.	30 mL
Water	3 tbsp.	50 mL
Fine dry bread crumbs	1/2 cup	125 mL
Chopped chives	1/2 tsp.	2 mL
Poultry seasoning	1/4 tsp.	1 mL
Salt	1/4 tsp.	1 mL
Pepper, just a pinch		
Canned crabmeat, membrane removed	4 oz.	113 g
Cod fillets (or your favorite)	2 lbs.	900 g
Light salad dressing (or mayonnaise)	2 tbsp.	30 mL
Seasoned salt	1/2 tsp.	2 mL
Paprika	1/4 tsp.	1 mL

STUFFING: Heat butter in frying pan. Add onion and celery. Sauté until soft. Remove from heat.

Stir in next 7 ingredients, adding more water if needed. A handful of stuffing, lightly squeezed, should hold together.

Place 1/2 of fillets in pan just large enough to hold in single layer. Spoon stuffing over top. Cover with remaining 1/2 of fillets.

(continued on next page)

Mix salad dressing, seasoned salt and paprika in small cup. Spread over top layer of fish. Cover. Bake in 350°F (175°C) oven for about 30 minutes until fish flakes with fork. Serves 6.

1 serving contains: 210 Calories (879 kJ); 4.9 g Fat; 31 g Protein; 468 mg Sodium

Pictured on page 35.

GET TALKIN'

When developing a conversation at the family table, avoid starting a sentence with "Would" or "Did". These words make it too easy to answer with "Yes" or "No", the last words of many conversations. Starting conversations with "How" and "What" often leads to interesting discussions.

Fish Loaf

Every fish loaf is not salmon. Try this loaf in a casserole dish.

Diced potato	1½ cups	375 mL
Boiling water	1½ cups	375 mL
Cod or sole fillets or other	1½ lbs.	680 g
Butter or hard margarine	1 tbsp.	15 mL
Chopped onion	1½ cups	375 mL
Lemon juice, fresh or bottled	1½ tsp.	7 mL
Prepared horseradish	1½ tsp.	7 mL
Prepared mustard	½ tsp.	2 mL
Salt	1 tsp.	5 mL
Pepper	¼ tsp.	1 mL
Cream Sauce, page 150		

Cook potato in boiling water in large saucepan for 10 minutes.

Add fish. Cook for 10 minutes until potato and fish are tender. Drain. Mash together.

Melt butter in frying pan. Add onion. Sauté until soft and browned. Add to potato mixture.

Add next 5 ingredients. Mix. Pack in greased 1½ quart (1.5 L) casserole. Bake, uncovered, in 375°F (190°C) oven for 30 to 40 minutes until hot.

Serve with *Cream Sauce*. Serves 6.

1 serving with sauce contains: 223 Calories (935 kJ); 7.2 g Fat; 23 g Protein; 839 mg Sodium

Baked Fish

A mild tasty sauce dresses up this dish.

Butter or hard margarine	2 tbsp.	30 mL
Steak sauce	1 tbsp.	15 mL
Lemon juice, fresh or bottled	2 tbsp.	30 mL
Brown sugar, packed	1 tbsp.	15 mL
Soy sauce	1 tsp.	5 mL
Salt	¼ tsp.	1 mL
Fish fillets (cod, sole or your favorite)	1½ lbs.	680 g
Water	1 tsp.	5 mL
Cornstarch	1 tsp.	5 mL

Melt butter in saucepan. Remove from heat. Add steak sauce, lemon juice, brown sugar, soy sauce and salt. Stir.

Dip fillets in sauce. Reserve remaining sauce. Arrange fillets on greased baking pan large enough to hold in single layer. Bake in 350°F (175°C) oven for about 20 minutes until fish flakes with fork. Remove fillets to plate.

Mix water and cornstarch in small cup. Pour juice from pan and reserved sauce into small saucepan. Heat to boiling. Stir in cornstarch mixture. Continue to stir until mixture boils and thickens. Pour over fish fillets. Serves 4.

1 serving contains: 212 Calories (886 kJ); 7 g Fat; 31 g Protein; 420 mg Sodium

Remember When?

One night ask Dad to tell the family about the funniest thing that ever happened to him. Everyone will begin to remember their own stories and dinner can quickly become an hysterical feast!

Tuna Supper

Contains peas, carrots and noodles. Topped with crunchy onion rings.

Water (or milk)	¼ cup	60 mL
Condensed cream of mushroom soup	10 oz.	284 mL
Canned flaked tuna in water, drained	6½ oz.	184 g
Frozen peas and carrots	2 cups	500 mL
Canned sliced mushrooms, drained	10 oz.	284 mL
Dry onion flakes	1 tbsp.	15 mL
Chow mein noodles	1 cup	250 mL
Canned french-fried onions	2¾ oz.	79 g

Stir water and soup together in bowl.

Add next 5 ingredients. Stir. Turn into ungreased 1½ quart (1.5 L) casserole.

Cover with onion rings. Bake, uncovered, in 350°F (175°C) oven for about 35 minutes. Check onion rings at half time. If too crisp, cover casserole. Serves 4.

1 serving contains: 307 Calories (1285 kJ); 12.9 g Fat; 20 g Protein; 1133 mg Sodium

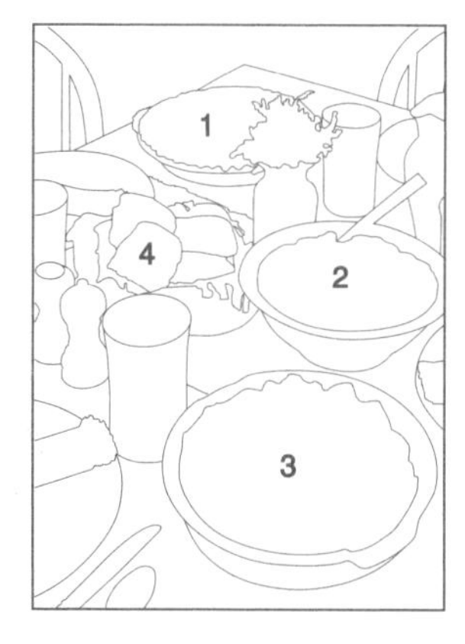

1. Crumb Pie, page 98
2. Mashed Potatoes, page 152
3. Porcupines, page 75
4. Southern Raised Biscuits, page 14

Pottery dishes courtesy of: Clayworks Studios
Salt/pepper shakers and table runner courtesy of: Enchanted Kitchen
Cutlery courtesy of: Stokes
Vase courtesy of: Mystique Pottery & Gifts
Chairs courtesy of: United Furniture Warehouse

Punch In A Pitcher

Looks like sunshine. Not too sweet. Serve by the pitcherful or serve in a punch bowl.

Frozen concentrated orange juice, thawed	6 oz.	170 g
Frozen concentrated lemonade, thawed	6 oz.	170 g
Grapefruit juice	2 cups	500 mL
Pineapple juice	2 cups	500 mL
Water	3 cups	750 mL
Ginger ale, chilled	2 qts.	2 L
Ice cubes, to fill glasses		

Combine first 5 ingredients in large container. Chill in refrigerator until ready to serve.

Use a punch bowl or 2 pitchers. If using pitchers, divide refrigerated mixture between them, adding 1 qt. (1 L) ginger ale to each. If using punch bowl, add full amount of ginger ale. Stir lightly. Pour over ice cubes in glasses. Makes 16½ cups (4.1 L).

½ cup (125 mL) contains: 54 Calories (225 kJ); 0.1 g Fat; trace Protein; 5 mg Sodium

Pictured on page 107.

Get Talkin'

Many families are interested in current events and enjoy reading the paper. If this is the case with your family, encourage them to bring a current event topic to the table for discussion.

Tomato Juice Cocktail

Lightly spiced. Always a good extra.

Tomato juice	4 cups	1 L
Worcestershire sauce	½ tsp.	2 mL
Celery salt	¼ tsp.	1 mL
Hot pepper sauce	⅛ tsp.	0.5 mL

Pour tomato juice into pitcher. Add Worcestershire sauce, celery salt and hot pepper sauce. Stir. Chill until needed. Makes 4 cups (1 L).

1 cup (250 mL) contains: 43 Calories (181 kJ); 0.2 g Fat; 2 g Protein; 1014 mg Sodium

Variation: Omit hot pepper sauce. Add ½ tsp. (2 mL) onion powder.

Get Talkin'

Storytelling is a great way to get the family talking. Children of all ages love stories, especially ones about their parents. An embarrassing moment in a parent's life can open up the door to laughter and understanding.

After-Church Fondue

This is a fun, relaxing meal. Everything can be prepared ahead.
Just reheat sauce when ready.

Fondue Sauce

Condensed cream of mushroom soup	2 x 10 oz.	2 x 284 mL
Grated sharp Cheddar cheese	2 cups	500 mL
Non-fat sour cream	½ cup	125 mL
Chopped chives	2 tbsp.	30 mL

Dippers

Apple slices, bread cubes, cubed ham, wiener cubes, cooked potato cubes, cooked sausage cubes, cauliflower and broccoli (cooked tender-crisp)

Fondue Sauce: Put all 4 ingredients into double boiler or heavy saucepan. Stir often as cheese mixture heats and smooths out. When hot, pour into fondue pot over low heat. Makes 4 cups (1 L).

Dippers: Arrange dippers in bowls in center of table surrounding fondue pot. Set plates and dipping forks at appropriate places. Serves 6.

⅙ Fondue Sauce contains: 269 Calories (1124 kJ); 20.8 g Fat; 12 g Protein; 1604 mg Sodium

Variation: Add 1 tsp. (5 mL) onion powder, or add 1 tsp. (5 mL) Worcestershire sauce. For extra heat add about ¼ tsp. (1 mL) cayenne pepper.

ANGEL PASTA

Fine pasta sauced with a subtle flavor. Different from the usual.

Apple juice	½ cup	125 mL
Medium tomato, seeded and chopped	1	1
Sweet basil	½ tsp.	2 mL
Garlic powder	½ tsp.	2 mL
Lemon juice, fresh or bottled	1 tsp.	5 mL
Salt, sprinkle		
Pepper, sprinkle		
PASTA		
Angel hair pasta	8 oz.	250 g
Boiling water	3 qts.	3 L
Cooking oil (optional)	1 tbsp.	15 mL
Salt	2 tsp.	10 mL
Grated Parmesan cheese, sprinkle		

Boil apple juice in saucepan until half gone to strengthen flavor.

Add next 6 ingredients. Stir. Heat slowly while pasta cooks.

PASTA: Cook pasta in boiling water, cooking oil and salt in large uncovered pot for 30 to 60 seconds until tender but firm. Drain. Return pasta to pot. Add hot tomato mixture. Stir. Turn into serving bowl. Sprinkle with Parmesan cheese. Makes 4 cups (1 L).

1 cup (250 mL) contains: 256 Calories (1071 kJ); 1.1 g Fat; 8 g Protein; 871 mg Sodium

MACARONI AND CHEESE

Colorful with a lot of appeal. Red and green bits show nicely.

Elbow macaroni	2 cups	500 mL
Boiling water	2½ cups	625 mL
Cooking oil (optional)	1 tbsp.	15 mL
Salt (optional)	2 tsp.	10 mL
Finely chopped onion	⅓ cup	75 mL
Finely chopped green pepper	⅓ cup	75 mL
Condensed cream of mushroom soup	10 oz.	284 mL
Light salad dressing (or mayonnaise)	⅔ cup	150 mL
Jar chopped pimiento (2½ tbsp., 37 mL)	2 oz.	55 g
Grated medium Cheddar cheese	2 cups	500 mL

Cook macaroni in boiling water, cooking oil and salt in large uncovered pot for 5 to 7 minutes until tender but firm. Drain. Return macaroni to pot.

Sauté onion and green pepper in non-stick frying pan until soft. Add to macaroni.

Put soup and salad dressing into bowl. Stir vigorously. Add pimiento and cheese. Stir. Add to macaroni. Stir. Turn into ungreased 2 qt. (2 L) casserole. Bake, uncovered, in 350°F (175°C) oven for about 30 minutes until heated through. Serves 6.

1 serving contains: 436 Calories (1823 kJ); 24.7 g Fat; 16 g Protein; 871 mg Sodium

Mushroom Quiche

Golden brown and so tasty.

Butter or hard margarine	1 tsp.	5 mL
Sliced fresh mushrooms	4 cups	1 L
Chopped onion	½ cup	125 mL
Skim evaporated milk (small can)	⅔ cup	150 mL
Large eggs	3	3
Worcestershire sauce	½ tsp.	2 mL
Grated medium Cheddar cheese	½ cup	125 mL
Salt	¼ tsp.	1 mL
Pepper	⅛ tsp.	0.5 mL
Unbaked 9 inch (22 cm) pie shell	1	1
Grated medium Cheddar cheese	½ cup	125 mL
Paprika, sprinkle		

Melt butter in frying pan. Add mushrooms and onion. Sauté until soft. You may need to do in 2 batches. Cool.

Measure next 6 ingredients into blender. Process until smooth.

Turn cooled mushroom mixture into pie shell. Pour blender contents over top.

Sprinkle with second amount of cheese and paprika. Bake on bottom shelf in 400°F (205°C) oven for 15 minutes. Reduce heat to 325°F (160°C). Continue to bake for 25 to 35 minutes. A knife inserted near center should come out clean. Makes 6 servings.

1 serving contains: 315 Calories (1317 kJ); 20.1 g Fat; 13 g Protein; 501 mg Sodium

Creamy Pepper Pasta

The addition of red peppers adds not only color but a good flavor as well.

Cooking oil	1 tbsp.	15 mL
Chopped onion	1½ cups	375 mL
Garlic cloves, minced (or ½ tsp., 2 mL garlic powder)	2	2
Red peppers, seeded and chopped	2	2
Sliced fresh mushrooms	3 cups	750 mL
Salt	½ tsp.	2 mL
Pepper	⅛ tsp.	0.5 mL
White wine (or alcohol-free white wine)	½ cup	125 mL
Sauce		
All-purpose flour	¼ cup	60 mL
Salt	½ tsp.	2 mL
Milk	1½ cups	375 mL
Pasta		
Broad egg noodles	1 lb.	454 g
Boiling water	4 qts.	4 L
Cooking oil (optional)	1 tbsp.	15 mL
Salt (optional)	2 tsp.	10 mL

Heat cooking oil in frying pan. Add onion and garlic. Sauté for 3 minutes until onion is soft.

Add peppers, mushrooms, salt and pepper. Sauté for 3 minutes.

Add wine. Cover. Simmer for 5 to 6 minutes. Remove from heat.

SAUCE: Measure flour and salt into saucepan. Slowly whisk in milk until no lumps remain. Heat and stir until boiling. Add to vegetable mixture. Stir. Keep hot while pasta cooks.

(continued on next page)

PASTA: Cook noodles in boiling water, cooking oil and salt in large uncovered pot for 5 to 7 minutes until tender but firm. Drain. Serve sauce over pasta. Serves 4 to 6.

1/4 recipe contains: 605 Calories (2533 kJ); 9.8 g Fat; 22 g Protein; 757 mg Sodium

GET TALKIN'

A good exercise for children of all ages is to put some object on the table that looks different on all sides. Have each person at the table describe what they see. Even though the descriptions are different, everyone is seeing the same thing. The truth about the object on the table is a combination of everyone's perspective. This can lead to important conversations about the value of respecting other people's opinions.

PIES

Nothing says home more than a pie warming in the oven. Have the family cut their own shapes out of the leftover pastry dough and then add it to the top of the pie. If calories are a concern, cut slightly smaller wedges and add a slice of fresh fruit. Use light frozen yogurt in place of ice cream.

CRUMB PIE

This tastes like mince pie. It is so good and no one will be able to tell the difference.

Granulated sugar	1½ cups	375 mL
Raisins	1½ cups	375 mL
Dry bread crumbs	1½ cups	375 mL
Ground nutmeg	¾ tsp.	4 mL
Ground cinnamon	¾ tsp.	4 mL
Ground cloves	¾ tsp.	4 mL
Butter or hard margarine	¼ cup	60 mL
Water	1½ cups	375 mL
White vinegar	1½ tbsp.	25 mL
Pastry, for double crust 9 inch (22 cm) pie		
Granulated sugar, for topping	¼-½ tsp.	1-2 mL

Measure first 8 ingredients into saucepan. Stir often as mixture thickens.

Stir in vinegar. Cool.

(continued on next page)

Roll out bottom crust. Fit into pie plate. Fill with cooled filling. Roll out top crust. Dampen edges of bottom crust. Place second crust over top. Trim. Crimp to seal. Cut several slits in top.

Sprinkle with second amount of sugar. Bake in 400°F (205°C) oven for 30 to 35 minutes until browned. Makes 1 pie. Serves 8.

1 serving contains: 605 Calories (2531 kJ); 22.4 g Fat; 6 g Protein; 501 mg Sodium

Pictured on page 89.

Timeless Tip

I read in a recent survey that 64% of mothers who work outside the home clean up the kitchen alone. Many dual income parents feel they do not spend enough time with their children. Since we all must eat and the kitchen must be cleaned up, why not do it together? It provides a great opportunity to continue the dinnertime conversation.

Cream Pie

Light in texture, heavy in flavor. Meringue topped.

Butter or hard margarine	1 tbsp.	15 mL
Milk	1½ cups	375 mL
Granulated sugar	½ cup	125 mL
All-purpose flour	⅓ cup	75 mL
Salt	¼ tsp.	1 mL
Egg yolks (large)	3	3
Vanilla	1 tsp.	5 mL
Milk	½ cup	125 mL
Baked 9 inch (22 cm) pie shell	1	1
Meringue		
Egg whites (large), room temperature	3	3
Cream of tartar	¼ tsp.	1 mL
Granulated sugar	6 tbsp.	100 mL

Combine butter and milk in saucepan. Bring to a boil.

Stir sugar, flour and salt together in bowl.

Add egg yolks, vanilla and milk to sugar mixture. Stir well. Stir into boiling milk until mixture returns to a boil and thickens.

Pour into pie shell.

Meringue: Beat egg whites and cream of tartar together in bowl until fairly stiff. Beat in sugar gradually until stiff. Spread over filling, touching edge of crust all around. Bake in 350°F (175°C) oven for 10 to 11 minutes until browned. Makes 1 pie. Serves 8.

1 serving contains: 289 Calories (1210 kJ); 11.6 g Fat; 6 g Protein; 305 mg Sodium

Banana Sour Cream Pie

A rich tasting dessert. Best eaten the same day. Can be assembled quickly if crust has been baked ahead.

Medium bananas	3	3
Baked 9 inch (22 cm) pie shell	1	1
Vanilla instant pudding powder, 6 serving size	1	1
Milk	1 cup	250 mL
Low-fat sour cream	1 cup	250 mL
Frozen whipped topping (such as Cool Whip) or whipped cream	2 cups	500 mL
Banana slices, for garnish		

Slice bananas into bottom of pie shell.

Combine pudding, milk and sour cream in small bowl. Stir vigorously to mix. Pour over bananas. Chill.

Garnish with whipped topping and banana slices. Serves 8.

1 serving contains: 273 Calories (1143 kJ); 10.8 g Fat; 4 g Protein; 231 mg Sodium

Get Talkin'

Sometimes reading a story can be the start of a great conversation. This is a fun way for your children to learn new words and develop reading skills at the same time. A few well placed questions can start many lively conversations. Be sure to recall a favorite story of your own.

French Mint Pie

Peppermint and chocolate–a perfect pair.

Unsweetened chocolate baking squares, cut up	2 x 1 oz.	2 x 28 g
Butter or hard margarine, softened	½ cup	125 mL
Granulated sugar	1 cup	250 mL
Large eggs	3	3
Peppermint flavoring	½ tsp.	2 mL
Salt, just a pinch		
Baked 9 inch (22 cm) pie shell	1	1
Frozen whipped topping (such as Cool Whip), thawed	1½ cups	375 mL
Grated chocolate	2 tsp.	10 mL

Melt chocolate in heavy saucepan over low heat, stirring often. Remove from heat.

Cream butter and sugar together well in large bowl. Add melted chocolate. Mix.

Beat in eggs 1 at a time. Beat well. Add peppermint flavoring and salt. Beat. Taste for mint flavor, adding 1 drop more at a time, if desired.

Turn into pie shell. Chill.

Spread with topping. Sprinkle with grated chocolate. Serves 8.

1 serving contains: 395 Calories (1651 kJ); 26.2 g Fat; 5 g Protein; 286 mg Sodium

Oatmeal Pie

A browned top with a custard-like bottom.
A good resemblance to pecan pie without pecans.

Large eggs	3	3
Brown sugar, packed	½ cup	125 mL
Granulated sugar	½ cup	125 mL
Butter or hard margarine, softened	¼ cup	60 mL
Corn syrup	¾ cup	175 mL
Water	⅓ cup	75 mL
Rolled oats (not instant)	¾ cup	175 mL
Medium coconut	¼ cup	60 mL
Vanilla	1 tsp.	5 mL
Salt	¼ tsp.	1 mL
Unbaked 9 inch (22 cm) pie shell	1	1

Beat first 4 ingredients together well in medium bowl.

Add next 6 ingredients. Stir well.

Pour into pie shell. Bake in 350°F (175°C) oven for 45 to 50 minutes. A knife inserted close to center should come out clean. Makes 1 pie. Serves 8.

1 serving contains: 447 Calories (1869 kJ); 18 g Fat; 5 g Protein; 1705 mg Sodium

Pictured on page 143.

Meringue Pie

Most refreshing as a dessert or as a snack with coffee. Just a hint of both lemon flavor and color.

Egg whites (large), room temperature	3	3
Cream of tartar	1/4 tsp.	1 mL
Vanilla	1 tsp.	5 mL
Granulated sugar	1 cup	250 mL
Cracker crumbs (such as Ritz)	1 cup	250 mL
Finely chopped pecans or walnuts	1/2 cup	125 mL
Topping		
Envelope topping (such as Dream Whip), prepared as directed	1	1
Lemon spread (available in jam section of grocery store)	1/2 cup	125 mL

Beat egg whites and cream of tartar together in large bowl until fairly stiff.

Add vanilla. Beat in sugar gradually. Continue beating until meringue is very stiff.

Fold in cracker crumbs and pecans. Spread in bottom and up sides of greased 9 inch (22 cm) pie plate. Bake in 325°F (160°C) oven for about 30 minutes until dry. Cool.

Topping: Beat topping as directed on package until stiff. Add lemon spread. Beat smooth. Spread meringue on top. Refrigerate at least 1 hour before serving. Serves 8.

1 serving contains: 251 Calories (1051 kJ); 9.1 g Fat; 3 g Protein; 116 mg Sodium

Apple Pie

Serve this all time favorite with ice cream or cheese. Good warm or cold.

Pastry, for 2 crust 9 inch (22 cm) pie, your own or a mix		
Granulated sugar	1 cup	250 mL
Minute tapioca	4 tsp.	20 mL
Ground cinnamon	½ tsp.	2 mL
Sliced, peeled and cored cooking apples (McIntosh is good)	5 cups	1.25 L
Granulated sugar	¼-½ tsp.	1-2 mL

Roll out pastry on lightly floured surface. Fit into 9 inch (22 cm) pie plate. Roll out top crust.

Measure first amount of sugar, tapioca and cinnamon into large bowl. Stir.

Add apple. Stir well. Turn into pie shell. Dampen edge with water. Place second crust on top. Trim and crimp to seal. Cut slits in top.

Sprinkle with remaining sugar. Bake on bottom shelf in 350°F (175°C) oven for about 45 minutes until browned and apples are tender. Makes 8 servings.

1 serving contains: 351 Calories (1470 kJ); 15.1 g Fat; 3 g Protein; 276 mg Sodium

Ice-Cream Coconut Pie

Good flavor with a light texture. Easy to prepare.

Vanilla ice cream, softened	2 cups	500 mL
Milk	1 cup	250 mL
Instant vanilla pudding powder, 4 serving size each	2	2
Medium coconut	½ cup	125 mL
Baked 9 inch (22 cm) pie shell	1	1
Frozen whipped topping (such as Cool Whip), thawed	2 cups	500 mL
Toasted coconut	1 tbsp.	15 mL

Put first 4 ingredients into large bowl. Beat on low until mixed.

Pour into pie shell. Chill in refrigerator.

Spread with whipped topping. Sprinkle with toasted coconut. Chill until ready to serve. Serves 8.

1 serving contains: 356 Calories (1491 kJ); 16.4 g Fat; 4 g Protein; 271 mg Sodium

1. Raisin Date Balls, page 39
2. Sesame Cookies, page 36
3. Punch In A Pitcher, page 90
4. Tuna Sandwich, page 120
5. Thai Chicken Salad, page 111
6. Potato Salad, page 112

Glass serving dishes, dinnerware and cutlery courtesy of: The Bay
Glass pitcher courtesy of: Stokes
Glass bowl courtesy of: La Cache
Linens courtesy of: Le Gnome
Cabinet and chairs courtesy of: United Furniture Warehouse

Lemon Chiffon Pie

Delicate lemon flavoring in a delicate textured pie.

Envelope unflavored gelatin	1 x ¼ oz.	1 x 7 g
Lemon juice, fresh or bottled	⅓ cup	75 mL
Water	¾ cup	175 mL
Egg yolks (large)	3	3
Granulated sugar	½ cup	125 mL
Salt	¼ tsp.	1 mL
Egg whites (large), room temperature	3	3
Cream of tartar	¼ tsp.	1 mL
Granulated sugar	¼ cup	60 mL
Baked 9 inch (22 cm) pie shell	1	1

Sprinkle gelatin over lemon juice in small saucepan. Let stand 1 minute. Heat and stir to dissolve. Remove from heat.

Stir water, egg yolks, first amount of sugar and salt together in medium saucepan. Heat and stir on medium-low until mixture comes to a boil and thickens. Stir in gelatin mixture. Chill until mixture will mound slightly.

Beat egg whites and cream of tartar together in medium bowl until almost stiff. Beat in second amount of sugar gradually until stiff. Fold into lemon mixture.

Turn into pie shell. Chill well. Serves 8.

1 serving contains: 222 Calories (930 kJ); 9.4 g Fat; 5 g Protein; 258 mg Sodium

SALADS

Salads add that extra taste and color to the table as well as provide a variety of vitamins, minerals and other nutrients. The children can have fun tearing the lettuce while others prepare the vegetables and dressing. To save time during busy work weeks, wash and dry extra lettuce, store in airtight bag or container and place in refrigerator. Take out what you need as you need it.

GREEN SALAD TOSS

The horseradish adds a bit of zip to this salad.

Small head of romaine lettuce, cut up or torn	1	1
Green onions, sliced	3	3
Diced light Havarti or Edam cheese	1/3 cup	75 mL
Light salad dressing (or mayonnaise)	1/2 cup	125 mL
White vinegar	1 1/2 tsp.	7 mL
Prepared horseradish	2 tsp.	10 mL
Milk	1 1/2 tbsp.	25 mL

Combine lettuce, onion and cheese in large bowl.

Mix remaining 4 ingredients in small bowl. Pour over lettuce mixture using part or all as needed. Toss well. Serves 6.

1 serving contains: 99 Calories (413 kJ); 7.6 g Fat; 3 g Protein; 243 mg Sodium

Pictured on page 125.

Creamy Greens

Might look like caesar salad but dressed with a hint of blue cheese.

Small head of romaine lettuce (or assorted greens), cut up or torn	1	1
Marinated Onion Rings, page 154, (or slice 2-3 green onions)	10	10
Hard-boiled eggs, sliced or chopped	2	2
Crumbled blue cheese (to taste)	2-4 tsp.	10-20 mL
Non-fat sour cream	¼ cup	60 mL
Light salad dressing (or mayonnaise)	¼ cup	60 mL
Milk	2 tbsp.	30 mL

Combine lettuce, onion and egg in large bowl.

Mix remaining 4 ingredients. Add and toss. Serves 6.

1 serving contains: 105 Calories (439 kJ); 5.3 g Fat; 4 g Protein; 159 mg Sodium

Pictured on page 71.

Timeless Tip

Have you ever noticed that many of our possessions are described as being owned by certain members of the family? This is the children's room, or that's Dad's chair, for example. But ownership is never applied to the family table. It is a central place where family members gather, discuss, laugh, and share the events of their day. Treasure this shared place in your home and create shared mealtime memories.

THAI CHICKEN SALAD

Although dressing is drizzled over this salad, it may be tossed together and then sprinkled with the peanuts. A popular salad.

Cooking oil	2 tsp.	10 mL
Boneless chicken breast halves, skin removed (about ¾ lb., 340 g)	4	4
Small head of romaine lettuce (or other greens) cut or torn	1	1
Green onions, sliced	3-4	3-4
Chopped peanuts	½ cup	125 mL
PEANUT SAUCE		
Smooth peanut butter	3 tbsp.	50 mL
Soy sauce	1 tbsp.	15 mL
Cider vinegar	1 tbsp.	15 mL
Water	¼ cup	60 mL
Granulated sugar	1 tsp.	5 mL
Cayenne pepper (or to taste)	⅛ tsp.	0.5 mL

Heat cooking oil in frying pan. Add chicken. Brown both sides until no pink remains. Cut into short strips.

Divide lettuce among 6 plates. Sprinkle with onion, peanuts and chicken.

PEANUT SAUCE: Mix all 6 ingredients in small bowl or shake in jar. Drizzle over salad. Makes a scant ⅔ cup (150 mL) sauce. Salad serves 6.

1 serving contains: 246 Calories (1029 kJ); 14.2 g Fat; 24 g Protein; 261 mg Sodium

Pictured on page 107.

Potato Salad

Mix and let stand at least one hour in refrigerator to blend flavors. Colorful. Full of vegetables.

Cubed cooked potatoes (cold)	4 cups	1 L
Hard-boiled eggs, chopped	4	4
Grated carrot	½ cup	125 mL
Chopped celery	½ cup	125 mL
Green onions, sliced	3	3
Light salad dressing (or mayonnaise)	½ cup	125 mL
Sweet pickle relish	2 tbsp.	30 mL
Salt	½ tsp.	2 mL
Pepper	⅛ tsp.	0.5 mL
Milk, to thin	3 tbsp.	50 mL
Cherry tomatoes, quartered	6	6
Reserved dressing	1 tbsp.	15 mL

Combine first 5 ingredients in large bowl. Chill.

Mix next 5 ingredients in small bowl. Reserve 1 tbsp. (15 mL). Add remaining to potato mixture. Toss well. Spoon into serving bowl.

Spread tomato pieces over top. Drizzle tomato with reserved dressing. Chill until ready to serve. Makes 6 cups (1.5 L). Serves 4 to 6.

¼ recipe contains: 331 Calories (1383 kJ); 13.7 g Fat; 10 g Protein; 706 mg Sodium

Pictured on page 107.

Pineapple Slaw

A taste of the tropics.

Medium head of cabbage, shredded	1	1
Canned crushed pineapple, drained, juice reserved	14 oz.	398 mL
Light salad dressing (or mayonnaise)	½ cup	125 mL
Reserved pineapple juice	¼ cup	60 mL
Lemon juice (or more to taste), fresh or bottled	½ tsp.	2 mL

Place shredded cabbage in large bowl.

Add pineapple. Stir.

Mix salad dressing, pineapple juice and lemon juice in small bowl. Add to cabbage mixture. Toss well to coat. Serves 6.

1 serving contains: 109 Calories (457 kJ); 5.5 g Fat; 2 g Protein; 181 mg Sodium

Pictured on page 53.

Timeless Traditions

With children under twelve years old it is great fun to switch roles at the table. Let your children pretend to be another family member. Join in and take the role of one of your children. It is very interesting to see how children perceive their parents and how they act.

Tossed Salad

Dress this salad at the last minute to prevent sogginess. Dressing is flavorful.

Small head of lettuce, cut up or torn	1	1
Tomato, diced	1	1
Sliced celery	½ cup	125 mL
Radishes, thinly sliced	6-10	6-10
Green onions, sliced	2-3	2-3
Dressing		
Ketchup	⅓ cup	75 mL
Cider vinegar	¼ cup	60 mL
Granulated sugar	⅓ cup	75 mL
Milk	¼ cup	60 mL
Salt	1 tsp.	5 mL
Pepper	¼ tsp.	1 mL
Paprika	1 tsp.	5 mL
Onion powder	¼-½ tsp.	1-2 mL

Combine first 5 ingredients in large bowl.

DRESSING: Mix all 8 ingredients in small bowl. Makes 1 cup (250 mL). Pour about ½ cup (125 mL) over salad mixture. Toss. Store remaining dressing in covered container in refrigerator for future use. Salad serves 6.

1 serving contains: 64 Calories (268 kJ); 0.5 g Fat; 2 g Protein; 237 mg Sodium

Pictured on back cover.

MELON SALAD

Makes a colorful salad, one that you can also make into a breakfast shake.

Peeled and seeded cantaloupe cubes	1 cup	250 mL
Peeled and seeded honeydew cubes	1 cup	250 mL
Peeled and seeded watermelon cubes	1 cup	250 mL
Medium banana, cut up	1	1
Non-fat peach yogurt	½ cup	125 mL
Non-fat plain or vanilla yogurt	1 cup	250 mL

Arrange fruit in bowl.

Mix both yogurts in small bowl. Serve with fruit. Makes 4 servings.

1 serving contains: 123 Calories (516 kJ); 0.6 g Fat; 6 g Protein; 78 mg Sodium

Pictured on page 17.

MELON SHAKE: Place fruits and yogurts in blender. Add 1 cup (250 mL) crushed ice. Process until blended. Makes 3 cups (750 mL).

TIMELESS TRADITIONS

Many people today no longer give thanks before meals. But reconsider its worth–it unites everyone around the table and puts them in a common state of mind before the meal starts. Saying thanks to the person who put the dinner on the table is also nourishing for that person to hear and for the family to express recognition.

SANDWICHES

On a busy Saturday or after church on Sunday, sandwiches can be made in no time at all. If there's a large group, set up an "assembly" line to make preparation even quicker and then gather around the table to enjoy a leisurely lunch.

HAM BUNS

Very attractive served as open-faced buns.

Canned ham flakes, with liquid, broken up	6½ oz.	184 g
Chopped green onion	¼ cup	60 mL
Grated sharp Cheddar cheese	¼ cup	60 mL
Light salad dressing (or mayonnaise)	2 tbsp.	30 mL
Sweet pickle relish	2 tbsp.	30 mL
Hard-boiled egg, chopped	1	1
Hamburger buns, split	5	5

Mix first 6 ingredients well in bowl. Makes 1¾ cups (425 mL).

Spread about 3 tbsp. (50 mL) ham mixture on each bun half. Serve cold or wrap each in foil and heat in 350°F (175°C) oven for about 20 minutes until hot. Makes 10 open-faced buns.

1 open-faced bun contains: 143 Calories (597 kJ); 7 g Fat; 6 g Protein; 426 mg Sodium

Tuna Turnovers

These little packets are good eating. A great variation on the sandwich.

Canned flaked tuna, drained	6½ oz.	184 g
Hard-boiled eggs, chopped	2	2
Chopped chives	2 tsp.	10 mL
Dill weed	⅛-¼ tsp.	0.5-1 mL
Onion powder	¼ tsp.	1 mL
Condensed cream of celery soup	½ x 10 oz.	½ x 284mL
Tube refrigerated crescent rolls (jumbo)	8 oz.	318 g

Put first 6 ingredients into bowl. Mix well. Makes 1½ cups (375 mL).

Separate crescent dough into 4 rectangles. Scoop a scant ⅓ cup (75 mL) tuna mixture onto each piece of dough. Moisten edges. Fold over and seal. Arrange on greased baking sheet. Bake in 375°F (190°C) oven until hot and browned. Makes 4 turnovers.

1 turnover contains: 256 Calories (1073 kJ); 11.1 g Fat; 20 g Protein; 865 mg Sodium

Timeless Tip

A very important contribution teenagers and adult family members can make is to help with the family meal. Offering to stop by the store or staying in the kitchen until cleanup is done can give everyone additional time to share their day with each other.

Beef Dip Sandwiches

This is a lot of fun. Beef-filled buns are dipped into beef broth for every bite.

Rump or sirloin tip beef roast	3 lbs.	1.4 kg
Water		
Beef bouillon powder	1 tbsp.	15 mL
Garlic powder	1/4 tsp.	1 mL
Onion powder	1/4 tsp.	1 mL
Worcestershire sauce	1/2 tsp.	2 mL
Pepper	1/4 tsp.	1 mL
Salt, sprinkle if needed		
Hard french rolls, split	6	6

Place beef in small roaster. Pour water into roaster half way up roast. Cover. Cook in 400°F (205°C) oven for 15 minutes. Reduce heat to 275°F (140°C). Continue to cook for 3 to 3½ hours until very tender. Remove beef to plate. Cover to keep warm.

Measure liquid from roaster. You should have about 4 cups (1 L). Add hot water if needed to bring measurement up to 4 cups (1 L). Add next 5 ingredients. Stir. Taste for salt adding a sprinkle if needed. Divide among 6 bowls.

Slice roast and fill buns. Serve with gravy for dipping. Serves 6.

1 serving contains: 441 Calories (1846 kJ); 13.4 g Fat; 46 g Protein; 696 mg Sodium

Tuna Buns

Best served warm but may also be served cold.

Canned flake tuna, drained	6½ oz.	184 g
Hard-boiled eggs, chopped	3	3
Light salad dressing (or mayonnaise)	⅓ cup	75 mL
Chopped celery	½ cup	125 mL
Chopped chives	1 tsp.	5 mL
Onion powder	¼ tsp.	1 mL
Tiny process cheese cubes (such as Velveeta)	1 cup	250 mL
Salt	⅛ tsp.	0.5 mL
Pepper	⅛ tsp.	0.5 mL
Hamburger bun halves, buttered	9	9

Combine first 9 ingredients in bowl. Cover. Let stand in refrigerator several hours or overnight. Makes 2¼ cups (500 mL).

Fill buns using about ¼ cup (60 mL) tuna mixture for each. Arrange in roaster. Cover. Heat in 350°F (175°C) oven for 10 to 15 minutes until heated through. Makes 9.

1 tuna bun contains: 269 Calories (1124 kJ); 10.8 g Fat; 15 g Protein; 670 mg Sodium

Timeless Traditions

The family table does not always need to be at the family table. For a change of pace, spread a quilt on the floor in the family room and have an indoor picnic. Even in the dead of winter, you can turn up the heat, put your shorts on, and dream of warmer days to come!

Tuna Sandwich

A good combination of flavors from the different cheeses and tomato.

Sandwich bread slices, toasted and buttered	8	8
Flaked tuna, drained	4¾ oz.	133 g
Mozzarella cheese slices	4	4
Large tomato slices	4	4
Gruyere cheese slices	4	4
Alfalfa sprouts, large handful		

Cover 4 slices of buttered toast with tuna. Layer mozzarella cheese, tomato and Gruyere cheese slices on each. Broil until melted.

Cover with sprouts and remaining toast slices. Cut each sandwich in half. Serves 4.

1 serving contains: 362 Calories (1514 kJ); 17.7 g Fat; 25 g Protein; 543 mg Sodium

Pictured on page 107.

Variation: These can be heated in the microwave 1 at a time, if desired.

Get Talkin'

If you have teenagers you know it is sometimes difficult to talk with them. To get to understand them better, designate one night a week as "pizza night" and encourage them to invite their friends. See who can make the most creative pizza and who can eat the most. Lively conversations will soon follow!

Pizza Buns

These will quickly become a favorite for your whole family.

Lean ground beef	½ lb.	225 g
Chopped onion	1 cup	250 mL
Tomato sauce	7½ oz.	213 mL
Canned sliced mushrooms, drained	10 oz.	284 mL
Salt	½ tsp.	2 mL
Garlic powder	¼ tsp.	1 mL
Celery salt	¼ tsp.	1 mL
Whole oregano	1 tsp.	5 mL
Onion powder	¼ tsp.	1 mL
Grated mozzarella cheese	¾ cup	175 mL
Grated medium or sharp Cheddar cheese	¾ cup	175 mL
Hamburger buns, split and buttered (or toasted and buttered)	5	5

Heat non-stick frying pan. Add ground beef and onion. Scramble-fry until onion is soft and no pink remains in beef. Drain.

Add next 9 ingredients. Stir. Can be stored in refrigerator 3 to 4 days or freeze for long term storage. Makes 2⅔ cups (650 mL).

Spread each bun half with about ¼ cup (60 mL) ground beef mixture. Arrange on ungreased broiler tray. Broil until hot and bubbly. Makes 10 open-faced buns.

1 open-faced bun contains: 185 Calories (772 kJ); 8.5 g Fat; 11 g Protein; 600 mg Sodium

Soups

Bring the family together on a cold day for a delicious bowl of hot soup. Soup makes a nice light lunch or an accompaniment with the main course. A heartier, thicker soup or chowder served with a bun or biscuit is a great meal on its own.

Cabbage Chowder

Thick creamy soup with wieners that add to the flavor.

Condensed cream of chicken soup	10 oz.	284 mL
Soup cans of milk	2 x 10 oz.	2 x 284 mL
Coarsely grated cabbage	3 cups	750 mL
Grated potato	1 cup	250 mL
Wieners, tofu or regular, diced	3	3
Salt	1/4 tsp.	1 mL
Pepper	1/8 tsp.	0.5 mL
Grated sharp Cheddar cheese (optional, but good)	1/2 cup	125 mL

Combine first 7 ingredients in large saucepan. Stir well. Heat on low, stirring often, until boiling. Boil gently for 30 to 40 minutes until vegetables are cooked.

Add cheese. Stir. Makes 6 cups (1.5 L).

1 cup (250 mL) contains: 149 Calories (623 kJ); 4.2 g Fat; 11 g Protein; 741 mg Sodium

Chicken And Ham Soup

Quite a mixture in this tasty soup. Enjoyed by all.

Long grain rice	½ cup	125 mL
Water	4 cups	1 L
Elbow macaroni	¾ cup	175 mL
Chopped onion	1 cup	250 mL
Grated carrot	½ cup	125 mL
Condensed cream of chicken soup	10 oz.	284 mL
Canned ham flakes, with liquid	6½ oz.	184 g
Canned chicken flakes, with liquid	6½ oz.	184 g
Skim evaporated milk (small can)	⅔ cup	150 mL
Chicken bouillon powder	1 tsp.	5 mL
Salt	1 tsp.	5 mL
Canned tomatoes, with juice	14 oz.	398 mL

Cook rice, covered in water, for 10 minutes in large saucepan.

Add macaroni, onion and carrot. Cook about 5 to 7 minutes until tender.

Add next 6 ingredients. Heat until simmering.

Add tomatoes with juice. Heat until almost boiling. Add a bit more water if too thick. Makes 9 cups (2.25 L).

1 cup (250 mL) contains: 243 Calories (1018 kJ); 8 g Fat; 12 g Protein; 1096 mg Sodium

Timeless Traditions

Once a week pick a family member to prepare a simple dinner. Chicken And Ham Soup, above, is a great recipe for the "one pot cook" in the house who doesn't usually cook. It is delicious with Southern Cornbread, page 15.

Pea Soup

An easy quick method to make split pea soup. Very tasty.

Split green peas	2 cups	500 mL
Water	8 cups	2 L
Chopped onion	½ cup	125 mL
Grated carrot	1 cup	250 mL
Canned ham flakes, with liquid	6½ oz.	184 g
Salt	2 tsp.	10 mL
Pepper	½ tsp.	2 mL

Measure all 7 ingredients into large pot. Heat, stirring often, until boiling. Cover. Boil slowly for about 45 minutes until vegetables are tender. Makes 9 cups (2.25 L).

1 cup (250 mL) contains: 222 Calories (929 kJ); 4.5 g Fat; 15 g Protein; 894 mg Sodium

1. Apricot Squares, page 131
2. Toffee Squares, page 133
3. Corn Chowder, page 126
4. Green Salad Toss, page 109
5. Creamy Burritos, page 66

Dinnerware, glassware and cutlery courtesy of: Stokes
Serving platter courtesy of: La Cache
Linens courtesy of: Eaton's
Table courtesy of: United Furniture Warehouse

Corn Chowder

Sweet and excellent soup. Thyme adds a mysterious flavor.

Butter or hard margarine	1 tbsp.	15 mL
Chopped onion	1¼ cups	300 mL
Chopped celery	⅓ cup	75 mL
Grated carrot	⅓ cup	75 mL
Diced potato	1½ cups	375 mL
Water	2 cups	500 mL
Bay leaf	1	1
All-purpose flour	2 tbsp.	30 mL
Skim evaporated milk	⅔ cup	150 mL
Canned cream-style corn	14 oz.	398 mL
Ground thyme	½ tsp.	2 mL
Chicken bouillon powder	1 tsp.	5 mL

Melt butter in large saucepan. Add onion, celery and carrot. Sauté for about 5 minutes until soft.

Add potato, water and bay leaf. Cover. Simmer for 10 minutes.

Put flour into small bowl. Gradually mix in milk until no lumps remain. Stir into simmering vegetables until mixture returns to a boil and thickens.

Add corn, thyme and bouillon powder. Heat through. Discard bay leaf. Makes 7 cups (1.75 L).

1 cup (250 mL) contains: 131 Calories (547 kJ); 2.2 g Fat; 5 g Protein; 325 mg Sodium

Pictured on page 125.

MEATY SOUP

A meal-type savory soup. Serve with biscuits and a dessert.

Beef stew meat, trimmed of fat, cut into ½ inch (12 mm) cubes	1 lb.	454 g
Water	7 cups	1.75 L
Gravy browner	1 tsp.	5 mL
Chopped onion	1½ cups	375 mL
Grated potato	1½ cups	375 mL
Grated carrot	¾ cup	175 mL
Paprika	2 tsp.	10 mL
Parsley flakes	2 tsp.	10 mL
Ketchup	1 tbsp.	15 mL
Ground thyme	⅛ tsp.	0.5 mL
Salt	1½ tsp.	7 mL
Pepper	¼ tsp.	1 mL

Heat beef, water and gravy browner, covered, in dutch oven until boiling. Boil gently for 1½ hours. Beef should be very tender.

Add remaining 9 ingredients. Stir. Return to a boil. Cover. Boil gently, stirring occasionally, for 25 to 35 minutes until vegetables are tender. Taste for seasoning, adding more if needed. Makes 8 cups (2 L).

1 cup (250 mL) contains: 99 Calories (415 kJ); 1.9 g Fat; 10 g Protein; 580 mg Sodium

TIMELESS TRADITIONS

Family traditions are often the structure of a secure family, even in these times of rapid change. Whether it is soup on Monday nights or pancakes on Saturday mornings, food traditions can nourish us in many ways.

Chicken Noodle Soup

A snap to make. Noodles are added raw. A full soup.

Chicken bouillon cubes	7 x 1/5 oz.	7 x 6 g
Boiling water	6 cups	1.5 L
Thinly sliced carrot (small carrots look best)	1 cup	250 mL
Parsley flakes	1 tsp.	5 mL
Dry medium noodles (about 2 cups, 500 mL)	4 oz.	125 g
Canned chicken flakes, with liquid	6½ oz.	184 g
Soy sauce	1 tsp.	5 mL
Onion powder	¼ tsp.	1 mL

Dissolve bouillon cubes in boiling water in large pot.

Add carrot and parsley. Cover. Cook for 10 minutes.

Add noodles, chicken with liquid, soy sauce and onion powder. Cover. Cook for about 10 minutes until noodles are tender. Makes a generous 6 cups (1.5 L).

1 cup (250 mL) contains: 152 Calories (637 kJ); 3.1 g Fat; 11 g Protein; 1874 mg Sodium

Pictured on page 35.

Get Talkin'

Start your next dinner by asking everyone to compliment someone at the table. Sometimes we take each other's gifts for granted and miss opportunities to praise them.

Chicken Curry Soup

Similar to a chowder. An easy from-the-shelf soup. More curry may be added as desired.

Condensed cream of chicken soup	10 oz.	284 mL
Soup can of milk	10 oz.	284 mL
Canned flakes of chicken, with liquid, broken up	6½ oz.	184 g
Grated carrot	½ cup	125 mL
Minced onion (or 1 tsp., 5 mL flakes)	1 tbsp.	15 mL
Instant rice	½ cup	125 mL
Curry powder, large measure	½ tsp.	2 mL
Chicken bouillon powder	2½ tsp.	12 mL
Water	2 cups	500 mL

Place all 9 ingredients in large saucepan. Bring to a boil, stirring often. Boil gently for 10 to 15 minutes until carrot is cooked. If soup thickens on standing, stir in a bit more water. Makes 4 cups (1 L).

1 cup (250 mL) contains: 238 Calories (997 kJ); 9.3 g Fat; 16 g Protein; 1273 mg Sodium

Timeless Traditions

I know a family who has a fun wintertime tradition. Every Monday night from September 1 to May 1 they have soup for dinner. Many memorable family conversations have grown out of this simple tradition. They have gotten to enjoy gathering around the family table so much that their conversations often carry on past the normal dinnertime, even when it is not Monday night.

Sauerkraut Soup

The cardamom adds to the wonderful flavor.

Sauerkraut, rinsed and drained	28 oz.	796 mL
Water	10 cups	2.5 L
Tomato juice	2 cups	500 mL
Chopped onion	1½ cups	375 mL
Diced or sliced carrot	1 cup	250 mL
Beef bouillon powder	2 tbsp.	30 mL
Thyme	½ tsp.	2 mL
Parsley flakes	2 tsp.	10 mL
Pepper	¼ tsp.	1 mL
Canned flaked ham, with liquid, broken up	6½ oz.	184 g
Brown sugar, packed	½ cup	125 mL
Cardamom	¼ tsp.	1 mL

Combine all 12 ingredients in large pot. Bring to a boil, stirring often. Cover. Boil gently until vegetables are tender. Makes 10 cups (2.5 L).

1 cup (250 mL) contains: 132 Calories (551 kJ); 3.9 g Fat; 5 g Protein; 1060 mg Sodium

Timeless Traditions

Much of the fun of special events like holidays and vacations comes from the anticipation. Planning for the events around the family table makes for lively and excited dinnertime conversations.

SQUARES

For the family meal that needs only a bit of a sweet ending, a plate of squares with some fresh fruit is the answer. Squares are easy to make and keep well in the freezer. Line the pan with foil before baking for easier removal before cutting. A knife run under hot water helps to make a clean cut.

APRICOT SQUARES

Moist texture with a showy apricot look when cut.

Butter or hard margarine, softened	1/2 cup	125 mL
Brown sugar, packed	3/4 cup	175 mL
All-purpose flour	3/4 cup	175 mL
Chopped dried apricots	1/2 cup	125 mL
Medium coconut	1/2 cup	125 mL
Chopped walnuts or pecans (optional)	1/2 cup	125 mL
Large egg	1	1
Vanilla	1 tsp.	5 mL

Cream butter and sugar well. Stir in flour to moisten. Stir in remaining 5 ingredients. Turn into greased 8 x 8 inch (20 x 20 cm) pan. Bake in 350°F (175°C) oven for about 25 minutes. An inserted wooden pick should come out clean. Cool completely. Leave uniced or ice with *White Icing,* page 140. Cuts into 25 squares.

1 square without icing contains: 94 Calories (395 kJ); 5.4 g Fat; 1 g Protein; 45 mg Sodium

Pictured on page 125.

Dreamy Bars

Tasty and chewy. Coconut and chocolate chips show through.

Bottom Layer		
All-purpose flour	1 cup	250 mL
Icing (confectioner's) sugar	⅓ cup	75 mL
Butter or hard margarine, softened	½ cup	125 mL
Top Layer		
Large eggs	2	2
Brown sugar, packed	1 cup	250 mL
Vanilla	1 tsp.	5 mL
All-purpose flour	1 tbsp.	15 mL
Baking powder	½ tsp.	2 mL
Salt	¼ tsp.	1 mL
Chopped walnuts	1 cup	250 mL
Medium coconut	1 cup	250 mL
Semisweet chocolate chips	½ cup	125 mL

BOTTOM LAYER: Mix all 3 ingredients until crumbly. Pack in ungreased 9 x 13 inch (22 x 33 cm) pan. Bake in 350°F (175°C) oven for 12 minutes.

TOP LAYER: Beat eggs together well in bowl. Add brown sugar and vanilla. Beat.

Stir in flour, baking powder and salt.

Add walnuts, coconut and chocolate chips. Stir. Spread over bottom layer. Bake for 15 to 20 minutes more. Cuts into 54 squares.

1 square contains: 83 Calories (348 kJ); 5.3 g Fat; 1 g Protein; 36 mg Sodium

Toffee Squares

Caramely and chewy with a lacy appearance.

Butter or hard margarine	½ cup	125 mL
Corn syrup	⅓ cup	75 mL
Brown sugar, packed	¾ cup	175 mL
Rolled oats (not instant)	3 cups	750 mL
Vanilla	¾ tsp.	4 mL
Salt	¾ tsp.	4 mL
Semisweet chocolate chips	1 cup	250 mL
Chopped walnuts (optional)	¼ cup	60 mL

Melt butter in medium saucepan.

Mix in next 5 ingredients. Spread in greased 9 x 9 inch (22 x 22 cm) pan. Bake in 400°F (205°C) oven for 12 to 15 minutes.

Sprinkle with chocolate chips. Let stand a few minutes to allow chips to soften. Spread. Sprinkle with walnuts. Cuts into 36 squares.

1 square contains: 104 Calories (436 kJ); 4.9 g Fat; 1 g Protein; 89 mg Sodium

Pictured on page 125.

Timeless Tip

Few people enjoy cleaning the kitchen after a meal. It's amazing how much homework needs to be done immediately after dinner! Encourage everyone to stay in the kitchen until the cleanup is done. With everyone working together it takes very little time and the family learns how to work together.

Choco Pine Squares

Could be used warm as a dessert square or cold as a finger square.

Bottom Layer		
Butter or hard margarine, softened	½ cup	125 mL
Granulated sugar	1 cup	250 mL
Cocoa	¼ cup	60 mL
Vanilla	2 tsp.	10 mL
All-purpose flour	2 cups	500 mL
Chopped walnuts (optional)	½ cup	125 mL
Filling		
Granulated sugar	1 cup	250 mL
All-purpose flour	3 tbsp.	50 mL
Large eggs	2	2
Canned crushed pineapple, drained	19 oz.	540 mL
Lemon juice, fresh or bottled	2 tbsp.	30 mL

Bottom Layer: Melt butter in saucepan. Add sugar, cocoa and vanilla. Mix.

Add flour and walnuts. Mix. Reserve 1 cup (250 mL) for topping. Press remainder in greased 9 x 13 inch (22 x 33 cm) pan.

Filling: Stir sugar and flour together in bowl. Beat in eggs. Add pineapple and lemon juice. Stir. Pour over first layer. Drop dabs of reserved mixture here and there over top. Allow some pineapple to show through. Bake in 350°F (175°C) oven for about 45 minutes. Cuts into 54 finger squares.

1 square contains: 73 Calories (305 kJ); 2.1 g Fat; 1 g Protein; 21 mg Sodium

Pecan Bars

Small – but rich – bites of pecan pie.

Bottom Layer		
All-purpose flour	2 cups	500 mL
Brown sugar, packed	¾ cup	175 mL
Salt	½ tsp.	2 mL
Butter or hard margarine, softened	1 cup	250 mL
Top Layer		
Large eggs	3	3
Dark corn syrup	1 cup	250 mL
Granulated sugar	1 cup	250 mL
Vanilla	1 tsp.	5 mL
Salt	½ tsp.	2 mL
Chopped pecans	1½ cups	375 mL

Bottom Layer: Mix all 4 ingredients in bowl until crumbly. Press in ungreased 9 x 13 inch (22 x 33 cm) pan. Bake in 350°F (175°C) oven for 10 minutes.

Top Layer: Beat eggs together in bowl. Add corn syrup, sugar, vanilla and salt. Beat together well.

Stir in pecans. Spread over bottom layer. Reduce heat to 300°F (150°C). Bake for about 50 minutes. Cuts into 54 squares.

1 square contains: 123 Calories (514 kJ); 6.3 g Fat; 1 g Protein; 96 mg Sodium

Remember When?

Declare a night "family trivia night". How did Mom and Dad meet? Where was their first home? What is each family member's favorite dessert?

Zucchini Squares

A coconut and nutty taste with a flavor boost from cinnamon icing.

Butter or hard margarine, softened	½ cup	125 mL
Brown sugar, packed	½ cup	125 mL
Granulated sugar	¼ cup	60 mL
Large egg	1	1
Vanilla	1 tsp.	5 mL
Grated zucchini, with peel, lightly packed	1¼ cups	300 mL
All-purpose flour	1 cup	250 mL
Baking powder	1 tsp.	5 mL
Salt	¼ tsp.	1 mL
Medium coconut	½ cup	125 mL
Chopped walnuts or pecans	½ cup	125 mL
Cinnamon Icing		
Icing (confectioner's) sugar	1 cup	250 mL
Ground cinnamon	½ tsp.	2 mL
Butter or hard margarine, softened	1½ tbsp.	25 mL
Milk	4 tsp.	20 mL

Cream butter and both sugars together well in bowl. Beat in egg and vanilla.

Add zucchini. Stir. Add flour, baking powder, salt, coconut and walnuts. Mix. Spread in greased 9 x 9 inch (22 x 22 cm) pan. Bake in 350°F (175°C) oven for about 30 minutes.

Cinnamon Icing: Beat all 4 ingredients together in bowl. Add a bit more icing sugar or milk as needed to make proper spreading consistency. Spread over top. Cuts into 36 squares.

1 square contains: 97 Calories (408 kJ); 5.4 g Fat; 1 g Protein; 56 mg Sodium

Raisin Squares

Excellent. A new twist on matrimonial squares.

Bottom Layer		
All-purpose flour	1¾ cups	425 mL
Rolled oats (not instant)	1¾ cups	425 mL
Brown sugar, packed	1 cup	250 mL
Baking soda	1 tsp.	5 mL
Butter or hard margarine, softened	1 cup	250 mL
Filling		
Large eggs	2	2
Sour cream	2 cups	500 mL
Granulated sugar	1½ cups	375 mL
All-purpose flour	½ cup	125 mL
Raisins	2 cups	500 mL

Bottom Layer: Mix all 5 ingredients in bowl until crumbly. Measure out and reserve 1½ cups (375 mL). Press remainder in greased 9 x 13 inch (22 x 33 cm) pan.

Filling: Beat eggs with spoon in saucepan. Stir in sour cream, sugar and flour. Add raisins. Stir. Heat and stir until boiling. Cook for 5 to 10 minutes, stirring often, as it tends to clump. Pour over bottom layer. Sprinkle with reserved crumbs. Pat down with hand. Bake in 350°F (175°C) oven for about 30 minutes. Cuts into 54 squares.

1 square contains: 135 Calories (563 kJ); 5.3 g Fat; 2 g Protein; 71 mg Sodium

Nutty Chocolate Squares

A fairly light texture to this. Good chocolate flavor.

Butter or hard margarine	½ cup	125 mL
Brown sugar, packed	1 cup	250 mL
Milk	½ cup	125 mL
Large eggs	2	2
All-purpose flour	1¼ cups	300 mL
Baking powder	1 tsp.	5 mL
Baking soda	½ tsp.	2 mL
Salt	1 tsp.	5 mL
Semisweet chocolate chips	1 cup	250 mL
Chopped walnuts or pecans	1 cup	250 mL
Mocha Icing		
Icing (confectioner's) sugar	2 cups	500 mL
Butter or hard margarine, softened	¼ cup	60 mL
Cocoa	6 tbsp.	100 mL
Strong prepared coffee	3 tbsp.	50 mL
Vanilla	½ tsp.	2 mL

Stir butter, brown sugar and milk together in saucepan over medium-low heat until boiling. Remove from heat. Cool by placing saucepan in cold water, stirring mixture often as it cools.

Beat in eggs. Add flour, baking powder, baking soda and salt. Stir until smooth.

Add chocolate chips and walnuts. Stir. Turn into greased 9 x 13 inch (22 x 33 cm) pan. Bake in 350°F (175°C) oven for 20 to 25 minutes.

Mocha Icing: Mix all 5 ingredients in small bowl. Add a bit more icing sugar or milk as needed to make proper spreading consistency. Spread over top. Cuts into 54 squares.

1 square contains: 99 Calories (413 kJ); 4.8 g Fat; 1 g Protein; 88 mg Sodium

Caramel Crispies

Yummy rich crunchy squares will please young and old.

Caramels	24	24
Butter or hard margarine	¼ cup	60 mL
Milk	2 tbsp.	30 mL
Crisp rice cereal	3 cups	750 mL

Melt caramels, butter and milk in heavy saucepan over low heat, stirring often.

Stir in rice cereal to coat. Press into greased 8 x 8 inch (20 x 20 cm) pan. Chill until set. Cuts into 25 squares.

1 square contains: 69 Calories (291 kJ); 3 g Fat; 1 g Protein; 83 mg Sodium

Timeless Traditions

To continue the tradition of fun family meals for future generations, our children need to learn how to cook. It is never too early to involve children in the meal preparations. They will particularly enjoy helping to prepare their favorite dishes. Over the years they will learn by doing and carry the tradition of the family meal on to their families.

CHERRY SQUARES

Lots of cherry bits show up in this fine textured square.

Butter or hard margarine, softened	6 tbsp.	100 mL
Granulated sugar	6 tbsp.	100 mL
Large eggs	2	2
Almond flavoring	¼ tsp.	1 mL
All-purpose flour	1 cup	250 mL
Finely ground almonds	⅓ cup	75 mL
Baking powder	¼ tsp.	1 mL
Salt	¼ tsp.	1 mL
Candied cherries, quartered	⅓ cup	75 mL

CHERRY ICING

Icing (confectioner's) sugar	1 cup	250 mL
Butter or hard margarine, softened	1½ tbsp.	25 mL
Water	4 tsp.	20 mL
Cherry or almond flavoring	¼ tsp.	1 mL
Drops of red food coloring		

Cream butter and sugar in bowl. Beat in eggs, 1 at a time. Add almond flavoring. Mix.

Add remaining 5 ingredients. Stir until moistened. Spread in greased 8 x 8 inch (20 x 20 cm) pan. Bake in 350°F (175°C) oven for 20 to 25 minutes. An inserted wooden pick should come out clean. Cool.

CHERRY ICING: Measure first 4 ingredients into bowl. Beat well, adding a bit more water or icing sugar to make a spreading consistency. Mix in a few drops of red food coloring to make a pretty pink color. Makes a generous ½ cup (125 mL). Spread over squares. Cuts into 25 squares.

1 square with icing contains: 104 Calories (434 kJ); 4.7 g Fat; 1 g Protein; 69 mg Sodium

WHITE ICING: Omit flavoring and food coloring. Add ¾ tsp. (4 mL) vanilla.

Crispy Bars

A yummy icing covers a crispy center. This is m-m-m good. So easy.

Corn syrup	1 cup	250 mL
Granulated sugar	1 cup	250 mL
Smooth peanut butter	1½ cups	375 mL
Crispy rice cereal	6 cups	1.5 L
Icing		
Semisweet chocolate chips	1 cup	250 mL
Butterscotch chips	1 cup	250 mL
Smooth peanut butter	¼ cup	60 mL

Combine corn syrup and sugar in saucepan. Heat and stir until mixture boils and sugar is dissolved. Remove from heat.

Mix in peanut butter.

Pour cereal into large bowl. Pour syrup mixture over top. Stir well to coat. Press in greased 9 x 13 inch (22 x 33 cm) pan.

Icing: Place chocolate chips, butterscotch chips and peanut butter in heavy saucepan. Heat on low, stirring often, until melted. Spread over top. Cool. To hasten setting process, chill in refrigerator. Cuts into 54 squares.

1 square with icing contains: 131 Calories (550 kJ); 5.7 g Fat; 3 g Protein; 84 mg Sodium

Choco Peanut Bars

A melt-in-your-mouth square. S-o-o-o good. No baking required.

Butter or hard margarine, softened	1 cup	250 mL
Smooth peanut butter	1 cup	250 mL
Icing (confectioner's) sugar	3 cups	750 mL
Graham cracker crumbs	1½ cups	375 mL
Topping		
Semisweet chocolate chips	1½ cups	375 mL
Smooth peanut butter	1½ tbsp.	25 mL

Beat butter, peanut butter and icing sugar together in bowl until smooth.

Stir in graham crumbs. Pack into greased 9 x 13 inch (22 x 33 cm) pan.

Topping: Melt chocolate chips with peanut butter in heavy pan over low heat, stirring often. Spread over top. Cool or chill until firm. Cuts into 54 squares.

1 square contains: 125 Calories (523 kJ); 8.2 g Fat; 2 g Protein; 83 mg Sodium

1. Oatmeal Pie, page 103
2. Dilled Corn, page 153
3. Potato Casserole, page 148
4. Manila Chicken, page 56

Dinnerware courtesy of: Stokes
Pie plate and napkin rings courtesy of: Le Gnome
Cutlery and glassware courtesy of: The Bay
Napkins courtesy of: La Cache

MACAROON SQUARES

A real macaroon texture with chocolate chips. Not too sweet.

BOTTOM LAYER		
All-purpose flour	3/4 cup	175 mL
Brown sugar, packed	1/4 cup	60 mL
Baking powder	1/2 tsp.	2 mL
Salt	1/8 tsp.	0.5 mL
Butter or hard margarine, softened	1/4 cup	60 mL
Egg yolk (large)	1	1
Vanilla	1/2 tsp.	2 mL
SECOND LAYER		
Egg whites (large), room temperature	2	2
Cream of tartar	1/4 tsp.	1 mL
Granulated sugar	1 tbsp.	15 mL
Sweetened condensed milk	3/4 cup	175 mL
Fine coconut	2 cups	500 mL
Semisweet chocolate chips	1/2 cup	125 mL

BOTTOM LAYER: Measure flour, brown sugar, baking powder and salt into bowl. Stir well.

Add butter, egg yolk and vanilla. Mix until crumbly. Press in greased 9 x 9 inch (22 x 22 cm) pan. Bake in 325°F (160°C) oven for 10 minutes.

SECOND LAYER: Beat egg whites and cream of tartar together until almost stiff. Gradually beat in sugar until very stiff.

Fold in condensed milk, coconut and chips. Spread over bottom layer. Bake for 30 to 35 minutes. Cuts into 36 squares.

1 square contains: 90 Calories (377 kJ); 5.1 g Fat; 2 g Protein; 28 mg Sodium

No-Bake Summer Squares

With a bit of a crunch and not too sweet – but rich, nonetheless!

Butter or hard margarine	½ cup	125 mL
Corn syrup	⅓ cup	75 mL
Granulated sugar	2 tbsp.	30 mL
Cocoa	¼ cup	60 mL
Medium coconut	¼ cup	60 mL
Vanilla	1 tsp.	5 mL
Graham cracker crumbs	2 cups	500 mL
Icing		
Semisweet chocolate chips	⅔ cup	150 mL
Butter or hard margarine	2 tbsp.	30 mL

Melt butter in medium saucepan. Remove from heat.

Stir in next 5 ingredients.

Add graham crumbs. Stir. Press in greased 8 x 8 inch (20 x 20 cm) pan.

Icing: Melt chocolate chips and butter in heavy saucepan on low, stirring often. Spread over top. Cool completely. Cuts into 25 squares.

1 square contains: 128 Calories (537 kJ); 8.1 g Fat; 1 g Protein; 115 mg Sodium

Timeless Traditions

For many children, it is fun to hear about memorable events that happened to their parents when they were young. If you have any pictures of yourselves when you were your children's age, bring them to the table. Seeing pictures of their parents when they were young is great fun for children.

VEGETABLES

A meal is not complete without delicious vegetables. The children can help prepare by washing the vegetables. Depending on their age, they can also peel, chop, slice or measure. Participation in preparation may encourage participation in eating!

SAUCED PEAS

Peas are combined with zucchini and added to a mild nippy sauce.

Thinly sliced small zucchini, with peel	1½ cups	375 mL
Frozen peas	2 cups	500 mL
Water	1 cup	250 mL
SOUR CREAM SAUCE		
Low-fat or regular sour cream	¼ cup	60 mL
Light or regular salad dressing (or mayonnaise)	¼ cup	60 mL
Lemon juice, fresh or bottled	1½ tsp.	7 mL

Boil zucchini and peas in water for about 5 minutes. Drain.

SOUR CREAM SAUCE: Stir all 3 ingredients together in small bowl. Heat in microwave or in saucepan until hot. Add to drained vegetables. Stir to coat. Makes 2¾ cups (675 mL). Serves 4 to 6.

¼ recipe contains: 98 Calories (409 kJ); 4.1 g Fat; 4 g Protein; 166 mg Sodium

Pictured on page 53.

ORANGE-SAUCED BEETS

Excellent way to dress up beets.

Sliced or diced fresh beets (or 14 oz., 398 mL canned)	2 cups	500 mL
Prepared orange juice	1/3 cup	75 mL
Brown sugar, packed	1 tbsp.	15 mL
Lemon juice, fresh or bottled	1 1/2 tsp.	7 mL
Cornstarch	1 tsp.	5 mL
Salt	1/8 tsp.	0.5 mL

Cook fresh beets in water in saucepan until tender or heat canned beets with juice. Drain.

Whisk next 5 ingredients together in separate saucepan. Heat and stir until boiling and thickened. Pour over hot beets. Makes 4 small servings.

1 serving contains: 53 Calories (224 kJ); 0.1 g Fat; 1 g Protein; 134 mg Sodium

Pictured on back cover.

REMEMBER WHEN?

My friend's father loved words. At dinner he would choose a word and ask his daughter to guess the meaning of it. Sometimes she would be right and other times she would be hilariously off. After getting the correct definition, they would both use it in a sentence. Once in a while, she would contribute a word and try to stump her father. What a wonderful way to increase one's vocabulary–and it works for all ages!

Potato Casserole

Tasty and saucy.

Tiny new potatoes, with peel, or same size pieces of larger peeled potatoes	16-24	16-24
Condensed cream of chicken soup	10 oz.	284 mL
Onion powder	1/4 tsp.	1 mL
Grated medium Cheddar cheese	1/3 cup	75 mL

Arrange potatoes in single layer in ungreased 1½ quart (1.5 L) casserole.

Empty soup into bowl. Add onion powder. Stir together vigorously. Spoon over potatoes.

Sprinkle with cheese. Bake, uncovered, in 400°F (205°C) oven for 25 minutes. Cover. Continue to bake for 20 to 25 minutes until tender. Serves 4 to 6.

1/4 recipe contains: 221 Calories (924 kJ); 7.9 g Fat; 8 g Protein; 664 mg Sodium

Pictured on page 143.

Get Talkin'

One of the most revealing impressions of our family comes from the way we answer the telephone. Discuss at the table the way each person likes to be greeted when the phone rings and make your answering style a signature of your family. This simple discussion will generate greater awareness of the value of good manners.

SAUCED CARROTS

Spices are barely noticeable but add an extra boost.

Thinly sliced carrot, cut up in coins	4 cups	1 L
Boiling water, to cover		
SAUCE		
Prepared orange juice	⅔ cup	150 mL
Cornstarch	2 tsp.	10 mL
Brown sugar, packed	2 tbsp.	30 mL
Ground ginger	¼ tsp.	1 mL
Ground nutmeg	¼ tsp.	1 mL
Salt	¼ tsp.	1 mL
Pepper, sprinkle		

Cook carrots in boiling water until tender. Drain.

SAUCE: Whisk orange juice and cornstarch together in small saucepan. Mix in brown sugar, ginger, nutmeg, salt and pepper. Heat and stir until mixture boils and thickens. Makes ⅔ cup (150 mL) sauce. Pour over carrots. Toss. Makes 4 cups (1 L). Serves 6.

1 serving contains: 84 Calories (351 kJ); 0.3 g Fat; 1 g Protein; 187 mg Sodium

Pictured on page 35.

Creamed Onions

A homey way to dress up onions.

Sliced onion (quartered lengthwise and thinly sliced)	4 cups	1 L
Water, 1 inch (2.5 cm) deep		
Cream Sauce		
Butter or hard margarine	2 tbsp.	30 mL
All-purpose flour	2 tbsp.	30 mL
Parsley flakes	½ tsp.	2 mL
Salt	½ tsp.	2 mL
Pepper	⅛ tsp.	0.5 mL
Milk	1 cup	250 mL

Cook onion in water in saucepan until tender. Drain well.

Cream Sauce: Melt butter in small saucepan. Mix in flour, parsley, salt and pepper. Stir in milk until mixture boils and thickens. Add to onion. Stir. Makes 4 to 6 servings.

¼ recipe contains: 139 Calories (581 kJ); 6.8 g Fat; 4 g Protein; 435 mg Sodium

Get Talkin'

Many parents do not include their children in discussions about their jobs. Children often think that school is much harder than the "real world". Ask your children if they know what you do each day. Tell them about your daily routine and some of the challenges you face. This conversation is sure to create more understanding within your family.

Scalloped Potatoes

Canned soup and milk makes an easy sauce for this.
Add onion and you have a nice flavor.

Thinly sliced potato	4½ cups	1 L
Thinly sliced onion	1 cup	250 mL
Condensed cream of mushroom soup	10 oz.	284 mL
Milk	⅔ cup	150 mL
Salt	½ tsp.	2 mL
Pepper	⅛ tsp.	0.5 mL
Paprika, sprinkle		

Layer ½ of potato in ungreased 2 quart (2 L) casserole. Layer ½ of onion over top.

Stir soup, milk, salt and pepper together in bowl until well mixed. Pour ½ of sauce over potato and onion in casserole. Layer remaining potato and onion over top. Pour second ½ of sauce over all.

Sprinkle with paprika. Cover. Bake in 350°F (175°C) oven for about 1 hour. Remove cover. Bake for about 15 minutes until potatoes are tender. Serves 6.

1 serving contains: 165 Calories (692 kJ); 4.3 g Fat; 4 g Protein; 655 mg Sodium

Mashed Potatoes

A good make ahead. Simply reheat for delicious mashed potatoes.

Medium potatoes, peeled and quartered	6	6
Water, 1 inch (2.5 cm) deep		
Salt	½ tsp.	2 mL
Grated medium or sharp Cheddar cheese	½ cup	125 mL
Low-fat sour cream	½ cup	125 mL
Green onions, chopped	2	2
Onion salt	½ tsp.	2 mL
Pepper	¼ tsp.	1 mL

Heat potatoes in water and salt until boiling. Boil until tender. Drain. Mash.

Add cheese. Mash well.

Add remaining 4 ingredients. Mash. May be served now or refrigerated. Heat, covered, in lightly sprayed casserole in 325°F (160°C) oven for about 20 to 30 minutes, stirring every 10 minutes, until hot. Serves 6.

1 serving contains: 175 Calories (732 kJ); 4.9 g Fat; 5 g Protein; 87 mg Sodium

Pictured on page 89.

Timeless Traditions

Family traditions help us create the structure that gives our families a sense of security in this fast-paced world. Invite grandparents for a meal and a visit and ask them about their favorite family traditions. Ask them how those traditions developed and how they've changed over the years.

Dilled Corn

Depending on family size, you may need to double this recipe. Dill adds a nice flavor.

Canned kernel corn, drained	12 oz.	341 mL
Butter or hard margarine	2 tsp.	10 mL
Dill weed	½ tsp.	2 mL
Salt, sprinkle		
Pepper, sprinkle		

Heat corn in saucepan.

Add butter, dill weed, salt and pepper. Stir. Serves 4.

1 serving contains: 65 Calories (274 kJ); 2.5 g Fat; 2 g Protein; 211 mg Sodium

Pictured on page 143.

Lemon-Lime Cabbage

Gives cabbage a fresh sweet taste.

Small green cabbage	1	1
Lemon-lime soft drink (such as 7-Up)	1 cup	250 mL
Salt	½ tsp.	2 mL

Cut cabbage into quarters lengthwise. Cut each quarter into ½ inch (12 mm) slices. Place in frying pan.

Add soft drink and sprinkle cabbage with salt. Bring to a boil. Cover. Simmer for about 10 minutes until cabbage is tender. Serves 4.

1 serving contains: 67 Calories (280 kJ); trace Fat; 2 g Protein; 377 mg Sodium

Marinated Onion Rings

Try these in grilled cheese sandwiches or use in Creamy Greens, page 110.

Large red onion, sliced paper thin (use electric food slicer if possible)	1	1
Cold water, to cover		
Granulated sugar	¾ cup	175 mL
White vinegar	¾ cup	175 mL
Water	¾ cup	175 mL
Cooking oil	1 tbsp.	15 mL
Salt	½ tsp.	2 mL
Pepper	⅛ tsp.	0.5 mL

Separate onion slices into rings in large bowl. Cover with cold water. Let stand for 1 hour. Drain.

Measure remaining 6 ingredients into saucepan. Heat, stirring often, until boiling. Pour over onion. Press onion down under marinade. Cover. Let stand in refrigerator at least 24 hours before serving. Serves 10.

1 serving contains: 43 Calories (180 kJ); 0.7 g Fat; trace Protein; 68 mg Sodium

Get Talkin'

As a parent it is important to share stories of your life that reveal your fears and shortcomings. If a teenager is about to start a new job, he or she is probably feeling apprehensive and nervous. By sharing your experiences of your first job, you may reveal an understanding that reaches and encourages them on a different level.

Measurement Tables

THROUGHOUT THIS BOOK measurements are given in Conventional and Metric measure. To compensate for differences between the two measurements due to rounding, a full metric measure is not always used. The cup used is the standard 8 fluid ounce. Temperature is given in degrees Fahrenheit and Celsius. Baking pan measurements are in inches and centimetres as well as quarts and litres. An exact metric conversion is given below as well as the working equivalent (Standard Measure).

Spoons

Conventional Measure	Metric Exact Conversion Millilitre (mL)	Metric Standard Measure Millilitre (mL)
⅛ teaspoon (tsp.)	0.6 mL	0.5 mL
¼ teaspoon (tsp.)	1.2 mL	1 mL
½ teaspoon (tsp.)	2.4 mL	2 mL
1 teaspoon (tsp.)	4.7 mL	5 mL
2 teaspoons (tsp.)	9.4 mL	10 mL
1 tablespoon (tbsp.)	14.2 mL	15 mL

Cups

Conventional Measure	Metric Exact Conversion Millilitre (mL)	Metric Standard Measure Millilitre (mL)
¼ cup (4 tbsp.)	56.8 mL	60 mL
⅓ cup (5⅓ tbsp.)	75.6 mL	75 mL
½ cup (8 tbsp.)	113.7 mL	125 mL
⅔ cup (10⅔ tbsp.)	151.2 mL	150 mL
¾ cup (12 tbsp.)	170.5 mL	175 mL
1 cup (16 tbsp.)	227.3 mL	250 mL
4½ cups	1022.9 mL	1000 mL (1 L)

Dry Measurements

Conventional Measure Ounces (oz.)	Metric Exact Conversion Grams (g)	Metric Standard Measure Grams (g)
1 oz.	28.3 g	30 g
2 oz.	56.7 g	55 g
3 oz.	85.0 g	85 g
4 oz.	113.4 g	125 g
5 oz.	141.7 g	140 g
6 oz.	170.1 g	170 g
7 oz.	198.4 g	200 g
8 oz.	226.8 g	250 g
16 oz.	453.6 g	500 g
32 oz.	907.2 g	1000 g (1 kg)

Casseroles (Canada & Britain)

Standard Size Casserole	Exact Metric Measure
1 qt. (5 cups)	1.13 L
1½ qts. (7½ cups)	1.69 L
2 qts. (10 cups)	2.25 L
2½ qts. (12½ cups)	2.81 L
3 qts. (15 cups)	3.38 L
4 qts. (20 cups)	4.5 L
5 qts. (25 cups)	5.63 L

Casseroles (United States)

Standard Size Casserole	Exact Metric Measure
1 qt. (4 cups)	900 mL
1½ qts. (6 cups)	1.35 L
2 qts. (8 cups)	1.8 L
2½ qts. (10 cups)	2.25 L
3 qts. (12 cups)	2.7 L
4 qts. (16 cups)	3.6 L
5 qts. (20 cups)	4.5 L

Pans

Conventional Inches	Metric Centimetres
8x8 inch	20x20 cm
9x9 inch	22x22 cm
9x13 inch	22x33 cm
10x15 inch	25x38 cm
11x17 inch	28x43 cm
8x2 inch round	20x5 cm
9x2 inch round	22x5 cm
10x4½ inch tube	25x11 cm
8x4x3 inch loaf	20x10x7 cm
9x5x3 inch loaf	22x12x7 cm

Oven Temperatures

Fahrenheit (°F)	Celsius (°C)	Fahrenheit (°F)	Celsius (°C)
175°	80°	350°	175°
200°	95°	375°	190°
225°	110°	400°	205°
250°	120°	425°	220°
275°	140°	450°	230°
300°	150°	475°	240°
325°	160°	500°	260°

INDEX

A

After-Church Fondue 92
Angel Pasta 93
Apple, Baked 46
Apple Pie 105
Applesauce, Spicy 23
Apricot Squares 131

B

Baked Apple 46
Baked Fish 87
Baked Halibut 83
Baked Ham Steak 82
Baked Spareribs 78
Balls, Raisin Date 39
Banana Bran Loaf 13
Banana Sour Cream Pie 101
Bananas Caramel 51
Bars, see Squares & Bars
Beef
  Burger Meal 72
  Burgers 72
  Chili Con Carne 67
  Ground Beef Stroganoff 76
  Happy Day Casserole 68
  Meaty Soup 127
  Pizza Buns 121
  Porcupines 75
  Steak Stew 74
Beef Dip Sandwiches 118
Beef Noodle Bake 77
Beefy Rice Patties 70
Beets, Orange-Sauced 147
Berry Butterscotch 44
Beverages
  Melon Shake 115
  Pitcher Of Orange 19
  Punch In A Pitcher 90
  Tomato Juice Cocktail 91
Biscuits, Quick 12
Biscuits, Southern Raised 14
Bread Pudding 45
Breads & Quickbreads
  Banana Bran Loaf 13
  Cocoa Date Loaf 10
  Kiwifruit Muffins 16
  Quick Biscuits 12
  Southern Cornbread 15
  Southern Raised Biscuits 14
Breakfasts
  Buttermilk Pancakes 21
  Egg Casserole 22
  Souped-Up Eggs 18
  Spicy Eggburgers 20
Buns, Ham 116
Buns, Pizza 121
Buns, Tuna 119
Burger Meal 72
Burgers 72
Burritos, Chicken 60
Burritos, Creamy 66
Butter Icing 31
Buttermilk Pancakes 21
Butterscotch, Berry 44

C

Cabbage Chowder 122
Cabbage, Lemon-Lime 153
Cakes
  Chocolate 25
  Dated 26
  Lemon 27
  Plum 32
  Pumpkin 28
  Tomato Soup 30
Caramel, Bananas 51
Caramel Crispies 139
Caramel Sauce 51
Carrots, Sauced 149
Casseroles
  Beef Noodle Bake 77
  Chicken Rice 62
  Chicken Rice Bake 57
  Egg 22
  Happy Day 68
  Macaroni And Cheese 94
  Potato 148
  Quick Rice 62
  Tuna Supper 88
Cherry Icing 140
Cherry Squares 140
Chicken
  Creamy Burritos 66
  Crispy Oven 58
  Fast Chicken Tacos 55
  Honey-Glazed 61
  Lemon 65
  Manila 56
  Quick Rice Casserole 62
  Saucy 59
  Thai Chicken Salad 111
Chicken And Ham Soup 123
Chicken Burritos 60
Chicken Cheap Cheap 63
Chicken Curry Soup 129
Chicken Noodle Soup 128
Chicken Parmesan 64
Chicken Rice Bake 57
Chicken Rice Casserole 62
Chicken Rolls 54
Chili Con Carne 67
Choco Peanut Bars 142
Choco Pine Squares 134
Chocolate Cake 25
Chocolate Icing 24
Chocolate Sauce 49
Chowder, Cabbage 122
Chowder, Corn 126
Cinnamon Icing 136
Cobbler, Pear 48
Cocktail, Tomato Juice 91
Cocoa Date Loaf 10
Cod, Crab-Stuffed 84
Coffee Whip 47
Cookies
  Drop 33
  Lemon Oat 41
  Oatmeal 40
  Raisin Date Balls 39
  Sesame 36
  Speedy Chip 34
  Sugar 38
Corn Chowder 126
Corn, Dilled 153
Cornbread, Southern 15
Crab-Stuffed Cod 84
Cranberry Pork Chops 79
Cream Cheese Icing 28
Cream Pie 100
Cream Sauce 150
Creamed Onions 150
Creamy Burritos 66
Creamy Greens 110
Creamy Pepper Pasta 96
Crispy Bars 141
Crispy Oven Chicken 58
Crumb Pie 98
Curry Soup, Chicken 129

D

Dated Cake 26
Desserts
  Baked Apple 46
  Bananas Caramel 51
  Berry Butterscotch 44
  Bread Pudding 45
  Chocolate Sauce 49
  Coffee Whip 47
  Fruity Pudding 42
  Instant 52

Lemon Sauce 50
Pear Cobbler 48
Tampered Rice Pudding 43
Dilled Corn 153
Dreamy Bars 132
Drop Cookies 33

E

Egg Casserole 22
Eggburgers, Spicy 20
Eggs
Kids' Quiche 81
Mushroom Quiche 95
Souped-Up 18
Spicy Eggburgers 20

F

Fast Chicken Tacos 55
Fish & Seafood
Baked 87
Baked Halibut 83
Crab-Stuffed Cod 84
Tuna Buns 119
Tuna Sandwich 120
Tuna Supper 88
Tuna Turnovers 117
Fish Loaf 86
Fondue, After-Church 92
Fondue Sauce 92
French Mint Pie 102
Fries, Oven 72
Fruity Pudding 42

G

Green Salad Toss 109
Ground Beef Stroganoff 76

H

Halibut, Baked 83
Ham Buns 116
Ham Soup, Chicken And 123
Ham Steak, Baked 82
Happy Day Casserole 68
Honey-Glazed Chicken 61

I

Ice-Cream Coconut Pie 106
Icings
Butter 31
Cherry 140
Chocolate 24
Cinnamon 136
Cream Cheese 28
Lemon 27
Mocha 138
White 140
Instant Dessert 52

K

Kids' Quiche 81
Kiwifruit Muffins 16

L

Lemon Cake 27
Lemon Chicken 65
Lemon Chiffon Pie 108
Lemon Icing 27
Lemon Oat Cookies 41
Lemon Sauce 50
Lemon-Lime Cabbage 153
Loaf, Banana Bran 13
Loaf, Cocoa Date 10
Loaf, Fish 86

M

Macaroni And Cheese 94
Macaroon Squares 144
Main Courses
After-Church Fondue 92
Angel Pasta 93
Baked Fish 87
Baked Halibut 83
Baked Ham Steak 82
Baked Spareribs 78
Beef Noodle Bake 77
Beefy Rice Patties 70
Burger Meal 72
Burgers 72
Chicken Burritos 60
Chicken Cheap Cheap 63
Chicken Parmesan 64
Chicken Rice Bake 57
Chicken Rice Casserole 62
Chicken Rolls 54
Chili Con Carne 67
Crab-Stuffed Cod 84
Cranberry Pork Chops 79
Creamy Burritos 66
Creamy Pepper Pasta 96
Crispy Oven Chicken 58
Fast Chicken Tacos 55
Fish Loaf 86
Ground Beef Stroganoff 76
Happy Day Casserole 68
Honey-Glazed Chicken 61
Kids' Quiche 81
Lemon Chicken 65
Macaroni And Cheese 94
Manila Chicken 56
Mushroom Quiche 95
Oven Pork Chops 80
Porcupines 75
Quick Rice Casserole 62
Saucy Chicken 59
Steak Stew 74
Tuna Supper 88
Manila Chicken 56
Marinated Onion Rings 154
Mashed Potatoes 152
Meaty Soup 127
Melon Salad 115
Melon Shake 115
Meringue 100
Meringue Pie 104
Mocha Icing 138
Muffins, Kiwifruit 16
Mushroom Quiche 95

N

No-Bake Summer Squares 145
Nutty Chocolate Squares 138

O

Oatmeal Cookies 40
Oatmeal Pie 103
Onion Rings, Marinated 154
Onions, Creamed 150
Orange, Pitcher Of 19
Orange-Sauced Beets 147
Oven Fries 72
Oven Pork Chops 80

P

Pancakes, Buttermilk 21
Parmesan, Chicken 64
Pasta
Angel Pasta 93
Beef Noodle Bake 77
Chicken Noodle Soup 128
Creamy Pepper 96
Happy Day Casserole 68
Macaroni And Cheese 94
Patties, Beefy Rice 70
Pea Soup 124
Peanut Sauce 111
Pear Cobbler 48
Peas, Sauced 146
Pecan Bars 135
Pies
Apple 105
Banana Sour Cream . . . .

Cream 100
Crumb 98
French Mint 102
Ice-Cream Coconut 106
Lemon Chiffon 108
Meringue 104
Oatmeal 103
Pineapple Slaw 113
Pitcher Of Orange 19
Pizza Buns 121
Plum Cake 32
Porcupines 75
Pork
Baked Ham Steak 82
Baked Spareribs 78
Chicken And Ham Soup 123
Cranberry Pork Chops 79
Ham Buns 116
Kids' Quiche 81
Oven Pork Chops 80
Pea Soup 124
Sauerkraut Soup 130
Potato Casserole 148
Potato Salad 112
Potatoes, Mashed 152
Potatoes, Scalloped 151
Pudding, Bread 45
Pudding, Fruity 42
Pudding, Tampered Rice 43
Pumpkin Cake 28
Punch In A Pitcher 90

Q

Quiche, Kids' 81
Quiche, Mushroom 95
Quick Biscuits 12
Quick Rice Casserole 62
Quickbreads, see Breads & Quickbreads

R

Raisin Date Balls 39
Raisin Squares 137
Rice
Beefy Rice Patties 70
Chicken Rice Bake 57
Chicken Rice Casserole 62
Rolls, Chicken 54

S

Salads
Creamy Greens 110
Green Salad Toss 109
Melon 115
Pineapple Slaw 113
Potato 112
Thai Chicken 111
Tossed 114
Sandwiches
Beef Dip 118
Burger Meal 72
Burgers 72
Ham Buns 116
Pizza Buns 121
Spicy Eggburgers 20
Tuna 120
Tuna Buns 119
Tuna Turnovers 117
Sauced Beets, Orange 147
Sauced Carrots 149
Sauced Peas 146
Sauces
Caramel 51
Chocolate 49
Cream 150
Fondue 92
Lemon 50
Peanut 111
Sour Cream 146
Saucy Chicken 59
Sauerkraut Soup 130
Scalloped Potatoes 151
Seafood, see Fish & Seafood
Sesame Cookies 36
Slaw, Pineapple 113
Souped-Up Eggs 18
Soups
Cabbage Chowder 122
Chicken And Ham 123
Chicken Curry 129
Chicken Noodle 128
Corn Chowder 126
Meaty 127
Pea .124
Sauerkraut 130
Sour Cream Pie, Banana 101
Sour Cream Sauce 146
Southern Cornbread 15
Southern Raised Biscuits 14
Spareribs, Baked 78
Speedy Chip Cookies 34
Spicy Applesauce 23
Spicy Eggburgers 20
Squares & Bars
Apricot Squares 131
Caramel Crispies 139
Cherry Squares 140
Choco Peanut Bars 142
Choco Pine Squares 134
Crispy Bars 141
Dreamy Bars 132
Macaroon Squares 144
No-Bake Summer Squares . . .145
Nutty Chocolate Squares 138
Pecan Bars 135
Raisin Squares 137
Toffee Squares 133
Zucchini Squares 136
Steak Stew 74
Stew, Steak 74
Stroganoff, Ground Beef 76
Sugar Cookies 38
Supper, Tuna 88

T

Tacos, Fast Chicken 55
Tampered Rice Pudding 43
Thai Chicken Salad 111
Toffee Squares 133
Tomato Juice Cocktail 91
Tomato Soup Cake 30
Tossed Salad 114
Tuna Buns 119
Tuna Sandwich 120
Tuna Supper 88
Tuna Turnovers 117
Turnovers, Tuna 117

V

Vegetables
Creamed Onions 150
Dilled Corn 153
Lemon-Lime Cabbage 153
Marinated Onion Rings 154
Mashed Potatoes 152
Orange-Sauced Beets 147
Oven Fries 72
Potato Casserole 148
Sauced Carrots 149
Sauced Peas 146
Scalloped Potatoes 151

W

White Icing 140

Z

Zucchini Squares 136

MAIL ORDER FORM

Company's Coming cookbooks are available at retail locations everywhere!

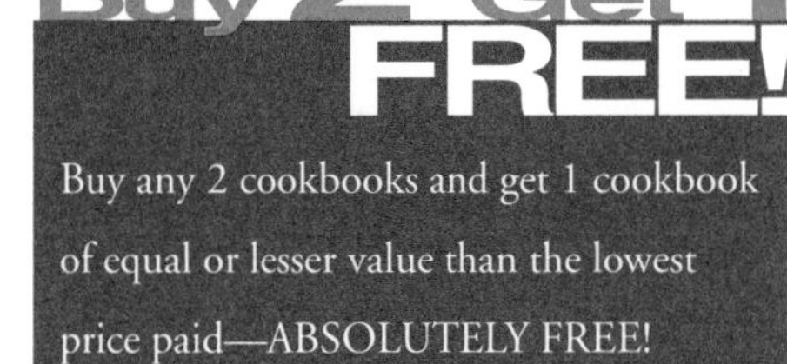

Buy any 2 cookbooks and get 1 cookbook of equal or lesser value than the lowest price paid—ABSOLUTELY FREE!

COMPANY'S COMING SERIES

Quantity		Quantity		Quantity	
	150 Delicious Squares*		Vegetables		Microwave Cooking*
	Casseroles*		Main Courses		Preserves*
	Muffins & More*		Pasta*		Light Casseroles*
	Salads*		Cakes		Chicken, Etc.*
	Appetizers		Barbecues*		Kids Cooking*
	Desserts		Dinners of the World		Fish & Seafood*
	Soups & Sandwiches		Lunches*		Breads*
	Holiday Entertaining*		Pies*		Meatless Cooking*
	Cookies		Light Recipes*		Cooking For Two*

** Also available in French*

No. of Books Purchased		Price			No. of Books Free
	x	$12.99	=	$	

SELECT SERIES

Quantity		Quantity		Quantity	
	Sauces & Marinades*		Ground Beef*		Beans & Rice*

** Also available in French*

No. of Books Purchased		Price			No. of Books Free
	x	$9.99	=	$	

INDIVIDUAL TITLES

	No. of Books Purchased		Price			No. of Books Free
Company's Coming for Christmas*		x	$19.99	=	$	
Beef Today!		x	$19.99	=	$	
The Family Table		x	$15.99	=	$	
Kids Only - Snacks*		x	$14.99	=	$	

** Also available in French*

- MAKE CHEQUE OR MONEY ORDER PAYABLE TO: *COMPANY'S COMING PUBLISHING LIMITED*
- ORDERS OUTSIDE CANADA: *Must be paid in U.S. funds by cheque or money order drawn on Canadian or U.S. bank., or by credit card.*
- *Rush courier rates available on request. Please call our Shipping Department at (403) 450-6223 for details.*
- *Prices subject to change without prior notice.*
- *Sorry, no C.O.D.'s.*

Bill my MasterCard or Visa (please check one)

❍ MasterCard ❍ VISA

Account # ______________________ Expiry Date __________

Name of Cardholder

____

Cardholder's Signature

____

TOTAL PRICE FOR ALL BOOKS	$
Plus Shipping & Handling (per destination)	$ 5.00
SUB-TOTAL	$
Canadian residents add G.S.T. / H.S.T. (7%)	$
TOTAL AMOUNT ENCLOSED	$

One low rate for shipping & handling—ANY SIZE ORDER!!

❍ **YES! Please send a catalogue.**

❍ **English** ❍ **French**

GIFT GIVING

LET US HELP YOU WITH YOUR GIFT GIVING!

- JUST GIVE US THE NAMES AND ADDRESSES of the people you wish to receive your gift, and we'll deliver them on your behalf.
- BE SURE TO SPECIFY the titles you wish to send to each person.
- IF YOU WOULD LIKE to include your personal note or card, we will be pleased to enclose it with your gift order.
- COMPANY'S COMING COOKBOOKS make excellent gifts. Birthdays, bridal showers, Mother's Day, Father's Day, graduation or any occasion ... collect them all!

SHIPPING ADDRESS

Send the Company's Coming Cookbooks listed on the reverse side of this coupon, to:

Name: ____________________

Street: ____________________

City: ____________________ Province/State: ____________________

Postal Code/Zip: ____________________ Tel: (   )   -

Company's Coming COOKBOOKS

Company's Coming Publishing Limited
Box 8037, Station F
Edmonton, Alberta, Canada T6H 4N9
Tel: (403) 450-6223
Fax: (403) 450-1857